*In My Father's House*

# *In My Father's House*

by William Prickett

The Cedar Tree Press, Inc.
Wilmington, Delaware
1993

Published by Cedar Tree Press, Inc.

*First Edition*

Published in a signed First Edition of 1,000. The first 25 copies reserved by the publisher. The second 25 copies are reserved by the author.

This is copy number ___45___.

Illustrations by William M. McCord

# Table of Contents

# Salutation, Foreword,
# and Note of Appreciation
# to You, the Reader

This is an outrageous Foreword to a collection of personal stories. If this description puts you off, then stop here and now. Close this book: give it away as the next wedding gift or hostess present or any sort of present that calls for a volume that is expected only to gather dust on the top of some library shelf or come to rest on a bedside table in the guest room. Turn on the television, watch the 11:00 o'clock news, or the last of the police thrillers. Perhaps it is time to put out the dog or brush your teeth, or turn out the light. I strongly urge the reader to do any one of these worthwhile things because I would rather part now with the reader on good terms rather than bad terms after he waded through this somewhat turgid little book. I may seek some time to publish another work. Perhaps we shall meet again under more propitious literary auspices. So hail and farewell to most would-be readers.

For those who are still with me, this, then, is a collection of very personal stories. The title is, of course, biblical, but also sort of catchy. I use it in part because it is the only one that occurred to me. More importantly, the stories in part deal with my father and his very strong influence on me. Like many fathers, he benevolently overshadowed me in my youth and, in fact, still does.

Thus, the thread throughout is my father. He figures in almost all of these accounts. However, as I look back over these efforts, I find that I have drawn a grotesque and almost ludicrous portrait of my father. I have left out entirely his serious side as a very good trial and appellate lawyer and a real student of the law. On the other side, I have written nothing about his wonderful sense of humor.

Freud wrote, "Anyone who writes a biography is committed to lies, concealment, hypocrisy, flattery and even his own understanding for biographical truth does not exist." More applicable is what John Cheever wrote in his private journal in 1961, "I have turned my eccentric old mother into a woman of wealth and position and made my father a captain at sea. I have improvised a background for myself—genteel, traditional—and it is generally accepted." How true!

There is a wonderful picture by the Spanish painter Velasquez in which he painted the children of the Spanish royal family. However, seen in a mirror is the faint outline of the painter himself. In a very real sense, any artist or writer says as much of himself as he does of his subject. Thus, Helga's World is not Helga's World entirely: it is as much a reflection of Andy Wyeth as it is of his model. In a very real sense these stories, I find, are reflections of myself.

Of course, my mother, a charming and attractive Belgian lady, also had a strong influence on me: if I have any manners or pretense to culture, it comes in great part from her. If I have no manners or culture or precious little of either, it is not her fault: she simply could not make a silk purse out of an ignorant swine. Still, it would not do, would it, to call the collection "In My Father and Mother's House"? Among other things, that would not make any biblical sense. Hence, Mother (if she cares at all, which she does not now and, in fact, probably never did) will have to forego whatever the pleasure or honor there is in being referred to in the title. (Perhaps, if there is a sequel, I could call it something like "Mother's Pearls," "Uncultured Pearls," or something equally cute.)

These stories were written at various times over the years. They have one thing in common. Like all authors of miscellaneous memorabilia, I really did believe that each piece was the best work since *Death in the Afternoon*. Where else to submit most of these stories but to *The New Yorker* so as to make them available to the readers of that publication? However, like scores of other unpublished authors, I invariably received the following short staccato printed notice of rejection in the self-addressed stamped envelope that is required when volunteering such amateur literary efforts to a prestigious literary magazine.

### *The New Yorker*

We regret that we are unable
to use the enclosed material.
Thank you for giving us the
opportunity to consider it.

### The Editors

Having failed of being published in *The New Yorker,* most of these stories wound up in *DELAWARE LAWYER,* the magazine of the Delaware Bar published by the Board of Trustees of the Delaware Bar Foundation. The stories had very little excuse for being published in that professional magazine except perhaps to liven its somewhat lugubrious content. In addition, I guess I had better "'fess up" in the interest of "complete candor," a legal principle that I have professionally advanced too many times to turn my back on now. I must disclose that I was and still am one of the trustees of the Foundation. Thus, there has been a total disregard of a most obvious and blatant conflict of interest, i.e., my literary goal of being published versus my duty as a trustee not to publish trivia or trash. However, conflicts be damned: I usually did manage to prevail upon my friend, the editor of that magazine, William E. Wiggin, Esquire, to allow these efforts to appear in print. Thus, these stories failed to get published in *The New Yorker* but did get published in a magazine of which I was a Trustee. It says something about both magazines, but I will leave that judgment to the discernment and taste of the reader. I do express my thanks to my fellow trustees for having looked the other way in originally publishing these literary efforts of a fellow trustee and now for graciously agreeing to allow me to republish all these efforts in book form.

It has been good form, I believe, over the centuries to include in the Foreword thanks to those who have contributed one way or the other to a literary effort. Thus, I again make my literary obeisance to William E. Wiggin, Esquire who was invaluable as my editor. Beyond that, I have to thank the ladies who patiently typed and retyped these efforts for me. Mrs. Margaret Malgiero and my secretary of many years, Mrs. Phyllis Zehr. Finally, additional thanks go to Vivian Coss for additional prescient comments and invaluable proofreading. Of course, it is also de rigueur to absolve all of the above of any responsibility, literary or otherwise, for the merits or demerits of the work. So be it.

It is also usual to dedicate a book to one's long-suffering wife. The office is now vacant. No dedication can be made to an empty office. Of course, the conditions of the office are tough: the past was checkered, the pay is nonexistent, the hours are long, the present is apt to be unpleasant, and the future is bleak. Therefore, I have had to look elsewhere for a subject to which to dedicate this work. But, ladies, do not despair. Simply because there is no present incumbent in my matrimonial seat does not mean that the undersigned has given up on ladies in general (or specifically) or turned his back on the fair sex. (On the contrary and aspersions to the contrary notwithstanding, any weaknesses lie on the other side of the equation, so to speak.) Therefore, to set all minds at rest and leave a small testament to the feminine gender, who are all too often neglected in this day of misguided equality, this work is dedicated to ladies generally. (That includes one-half of humanity.) Also, the dedication certainly should not offend those who, like the author, still think that God did right well with Adam's rib, for all women's original and continued frailties and failings.

However, on reflection, a dedication to all ladies, past, present and future, seems perhaps too broad. I am therefore tempted to narrow it to a smaller definitive list of females who have meant something very special to me. Such a list would include not only my old nurse, Rita, and two good hunting mares but, as well, a number of other ladies. (Those in the latter category know who they are, so there is no use publishing a list such as Leporello did for his wicked master.)

A word for literary critics and scholars: this work could well provide a host of nit-pics for those who have nothing better to do with their grant money than to parse each of these little sketches for factual and other inaccuracies, as well as stylistic and grammatical faults. But, as an artist is free to shade colors to get effect, or rearrange conventional forms to convey an impression rather than a photographic representation, so I write for pleasure, humor and impression, rather than an exact representation of what really happened. At times, the sequence has been rearranged, a fact is heightened or created or distorted as it has suited my fancy. Accuracy is my lot in the law, but not in this sort of affectionate nostalgia. Therefore, critics, scholars, and other pettifoggers, please lay off. All is admitted and beside the point. However, in issuing this broad disclaimer as to truth and accuracy, am I perhaps indulging in a latent phantasy that somebody is really going to take the trouble to try to sort out the truth as opposed to what I have written?

The profits, if any, from the first edition of this book will be donated to educational or charitable organizations. Why this gesture? In part, to curry favor with the public and in deference to the "Son of Sam" principle. Conceivably sales could contribute some needed funds to charities or educational institutions. Thus, these lighthearted tales of my education and upbringing might serve some useful purpose other than to wrap fish or gather dust.

I hope that you the reader will get pleasure and amusement from reading these stories just as I have gotten pleasure from writing them. Some readers appear in these accounts; others will know some of those who appear. But in any case, if you read these stories, you will end up knowing something of me and my father (and indeed others). On the other hand, though I will know some of you, I will not know all readers, but I would hope to make your acquaintance. I sign the copies of this small volume in part to express my appreciation and thanks to you who do me the honor of taking the time to read my stories. Therefore, please accept my thanks and appreciation.

But enough of these conventions, salutations, disclaimers and literary flourishes. If you are still with me, let's turn to the stories. As Edward DeVere, the seventeenth Earl of Oxford, wrote in *Hamlet,* "The play's the thing."

William Prickett                                                 New Castle, Delaware
                                                                        April 1, 1993

### *Errata*

Since dictating the above, a lady has agreed to fill my empty matrimonial seat. One condition was that I get this little work published. Her matrimonial and literary judgment are thus open to serious question. (Indeed, if I do not blaspheme, I am somewhat in the position of my fellow Princetonian: Zelda would not marry F. Scott Fitzgerald until *This Side of Paradise* was accepted for publication.) However, for what little it is worth, this volume is most affectionately dedicated to Caroline.

W. P.
August 7, 1993

*In My Father's House*

# The War on the Thistles

Recently, from my desk in the living room, I glanced idly up from my boring legal work to the corner of the pasture. I saw a tall thistle growing along the fence line. Its coarse, prickly leaves were surmounted by the flower, firm and slightly green but soon to become purple, then slowly turning white and dissolving into the seedy down that is carried away by the wind. As I glanced at the thistle, I could not help but think back on my father's war on the thistles. I guess that his war started in much the same way as my idle glance away from my work carried me to the thistle, except that he never made an idle glance in his life. He probably saw a single thistle and right then went and pulled it up. Perhaps he brushed against it or stepped on it and realized how disagreeable these weeds are. In any case, one hot June day before the war, when I was thirteen or so, I saw him working in the hot sun, pulling up some thistles. I asked him what he was doing and he said that he proposed to get rid of the thistles on the place. By this time, he had already determined that it would not do to cut a thistle's head off because it grew up again from the roots. He had also determined that one could not take the thistle by the stem even with gloves on because the stem of a thistle was simply too weak and broke off in one's hand leaving the stump to grow again. The only way to get the thistle out was to get some sort of a tool under the root, lever it up and then pull it up, root and all. It sounds fairly simple but it was actually quite a hard job because, unless one really got under the roots of the thistle, the thistle came apart and some of it was left in the ground and, as previously pointed out, it flourished again, seemingly with renewed vigor. A shovel could be used to get under the thistle but actually, my father, who was pretty thorough with any sort of a problem, came to the conclusion that there was one instrument that was particularly effective in dealing with these thorny pests. It turned out to be a heavy iron bar used many years ago for switching trolley tracks. It was about three feet long. One end of the bar had been pounded into a v-shaped point. The old trolleys used to carry them up front: the conductor would pull out the bar, jump down, switch the track over and then swing aboard the rear of the trolley as the motorman drove by. Just how my father had originally gotten one of these instruments I do not know since by then the trolleys had been replaced by trolley busses, but he found that these bars were most effective in dealing with the thistle. One took the bar and plunged it down next to the thistle and then pried up under the thistle, grabbing the thistle. It was a hot and disagreeable job. The thistle can only be located effectively in late June or early July when the telltale purple flower comes into view making it stand out apart from the other lush summer vegetation. On the other hand, thistling could not be done too late, since once the purple flower had burst open, literally millions of thistle seeds were liberated, each one of which would in turn produce another thistle. Therefore, the thistling season had to be in late June and early July.

Soon after my father resolved on his war on the thistles, he enlisted my twelve year old brother and me in the war, somewhat in the manner that Tom Sawyer got Aunt Polly's fence whitewashed. My older sister was occasionally conscripted. When my father found how effective his original trolley bar was but could not find any more at the old trolley barn, he got a puzzled blacksmith to duplicate the original one so that each of us would have one. Thus armed with thistlers on hot Saturdays and Sundays, we would fan out over the property and dig up thistles. Originally, we took entire thistles, put them in a pile, and burned the pile. However, the sheer number of the thistles made this ineffective. In addition, we found that when the thistles were burned, the flower would sometimes open and rising with the smoke would be a host of seeds providing next year's crop of thistles.

We then decided that we would uproot the thistle itself, cut off the purple head, and put the heads in burlap bags. The question then arose as to what to do with these collected thistle heads. They could, of course, be buried but they might germinate and sprout where they were buried and one would then have an entire forest of thistles—a thought too horrible to contemplate. It was decided in council that the bags of thistle heads would be loaded into my father's Chevrolet car and he would drop them at the city dump on his way to work. Of course, my father was busy with his law practice and it was sometimes several days before he would find an opportunity to get to the city dump. In the meantime, he would ride around in a car stacked up to the ceiling with bags of thistle heads. At times, some of the thistles would go to seed. I am afraid that he may have trailed thistle seeds out of the windows. Even today there are probably thistles around the countryside (and even in town) that owe their beginning to my father's inadvertent role as a Johnny Thistleseed. On one memorable occasion, my father had to go to a wedding at the Wilmington Country Club. Since he had not had an opportunity to dump his collection of thistles, the men of the parking service were greatly surprised when they had to park a small Chevrolet car loaded to the gunwales with thistles among the Cadillacs and foreign cars.

Actually, thistling was a hot and disagreeable job. No matter how careful one was, it was inevitable that one would get stuck with thistles as one went carefully through the steps of uprooting and decapitating them. However, the job had its own compensations. There was a sense of real accomplishment when, at the end of a long afternoon, one felt that a particular area of the property was completely free of the offending thistles and a sense of real triumph when after four or five disagreeable afternoons, it could be said that the entire property was free of thistles. After the first year's operations were completed, my father was justifiably pleased that he had rid the property once and for all of the disagreeable pests. He then would unconsciously cast around for some other project like disposing of woodbine or eradicating all the poison ivy on the acreage. However, when next spring rolled around, the telltale purple flowers again appeared. We, of course, banded together and thought that we would be able, at this point, to dispose of the few remaining thistles in short order: after all, it seemed to us that it was probably a task of diminishing magnitude and that, after a year or so of more work, there would be no thistles at all. We therefore, set to work and went through another four or five afternoons of thistling. These hot afternoons ended with a swim in the old ice pond and several well-earned beers. However, when the third year rolled around and thistles appeared in undiminished numbers, we all came to the slow realization that our war against the thistles was probably a hopeless or endless task. A moment's reflection told us why: while we were busy uprooting the thistles on our property, the gentle westerly winds were bringing the downy seeds from fields lying to the west of us, which our neighbors were not bothering to thistle. Indeed, in later years, as I rode over the fields and pastures lying to the north and west of us, I saw entire fields that had been unabashedly surrendered and had become under the sole dominion of the thistle enemy. However, our war against the thistles continued and dutifully each June we would sally forth armed with our thistlers. Of course, Mother, whose origin and temperament were Gallic, simply shrugged her shoulders at the war on the thistles: she never could fathom the strong Puritan forces that motivated or drove her American husband and his sons. She never could see why he never asked or (even thought of asking) the man who was hired to cut the grass to do or even share in this particularly disagreeable job.

When World War II came along, my brother and I were scattered to more serious wars and my father became too busy to thistle the place entirely. Still, from time to time, he would spend a solitary hot afternoon warring on the thistles. However, by the end of the war, Nature had quietly solved the problem of the thistles on the place: the fields had been kept cut and the thistles never got a chance to get started. In the second growth, the young tulip poplars and woods maples grew up and shut off the sunlight necessary for a healthy thistle. Still, here and there, throughout the property, a solitary thistle raised its purple head. To the end of his active life, my father always found the time to go to the tool house and get his trolley bar thistler, carefully uproot the offender, and cut off the head.

As I sit here and look at that arrogant thistle growing along the fence line, I have decided to declare war on the thistles on this place. (There is at least one rusty "thistler" lying in a corner in my own tool shed, and I know a blacksmith who could probably be persuaded to pound out some new orders.) I realize that, if I uproot the present crop of thistles, the prevailing winds will undoubtedly bring future generations of thistles from the uncut pastures lying to the west. My reason for doing so is far better than merely to rid this place yearly of the purple pest. While my son Will, who is taking his afternoon nap, is still too small to wield a thistler, the time will come when he can, and I want to try to instill in him, if possible, some of his grandfather's fierce joy in a hard task, the doing of which carries its own reward.

# *A Christmas Reminiscence*

A catalogue from a tree company in western Maine has arrived on my desk, as it does each year. As always, it evokes memories of Christmas when I was a boy and a young man. How so?

Well, for as long as I can remember, my father, a strict, hardworking lawyer all year round, would undergo a sort of change of character or metamorphosis in connection with Christmas. In place of his usual combative, assertive approach to life, people, and the law, he would become affable, genial, and sentimental during the Christmas season. Having changed his outlook and demeanor to conform with the festive nature of the Christmas season, he expected everyone else to do likewise. In a sense, this little account explains how and why my father's Christmas transformation and his yearly personal delivery of his homegrown Christmas trees appeared to fail in the end.

Actually, Christmas for my father would start each year in late January or February. At that time, he would write or call Mr. Tabor, then the Delaware State Forester, to place an order as a landowner for his small allocation of state trees. At that time, Delaware provided landowners with seedling trees, not for ornamental purposes but for reforestation, windbreaks, and Christmas tree production. Just how my father learned about this program I do not know. Be that as it may, my father always ordered about a hundred Norway spruce seedlings. This order would be delivered in late March or early April by the green State Forestry pickup truck. The order would consist of two dozen bundles of seedlings, 9 to 12 inches long, stoutly bound together by coarse brown bailing twine. At one end of each little tree, there would be the pinkish, naked root system and at the other end a spritely dark green plume of Norway spruce pine needles. The bundles of seedlings would be heeled in along the edge of the woods at some shady place at the property in Centerville. Then, on a blusterly Saturday or Sunday in late March or April, my brother, Harry, my father, and I would go out to plant the little trees. First, we would plunge two or three of the tightly bound bundles of seedlings into a pail half full of ice cold water. Then, each of us would take a long-handled shovel in one hand and a bucket in the other. Stepping along, we would thrust the shovel into the moist, frost-free, brown earth, pull the shovel smartly back, insert one of the stripling trees into the hole, and then carefully pull the shovel back out. With a firm stamp or two of one's boot, the new home of the little tree would be sealed up. Then one would pace six feet onward and repeat the process. In a year or two, these small seedlings would begin to peep above the grass and weeds. In five or six years, they would become fair size Norway spruces, just beginning to be right for Christmas harvesting. Of course, since my father planted a new batch almost every year and only gave out about forty or fifty trees each Christmas, there should have been an ever increasing crop of trees of various sizes. However, some of the little trees died, some were carelessly mowed down and others were choked by woodbine, honeysuckle, or just plain weeds. In addition, there were always some few people whose Christmas apparently consisted of coming out to the country to steal a Christmas tree. Indeed, on one occasion, someone even took a whole truckload of our trees.

Our problem from year to year was not big trees but to locate enough small trees to service the needs of our list of recipients. About ten days before Christmas, my father would pull out his little appointment book. In the very back of it, he had a penciled list of those who were to get Christmas trees and the size tree they requested. His list was made up of a totally diverse group of people whom my father considered as friends in the broadest sense. Thus, there were secretaries and former secretaries, social friends, legal and professional friends, tradesmen, relatives, and others. My father would go carefully over the list to determine whether there were any additions that he should make or whether there were people who had died, moved away or who had told him that they preferred to make other arrangements for their Christmas trees. When he had settled on the definitive list for that year, we three would sally forth on some December afternoon to tag selected trees with the names of the designated recipients.

Then came the prickly task of cutting down the marked trees. In order to do this, my brother and I would take on the tough job of burrowing through the lower branches to get into the interior of the tree itself. Once inside, one was in a kind of quiet little cocoon that had a sweet smell. A small timber saw was used to cut away the dead branches so that the tree itself could be sawed down. Usually, it only took a score of strokes with the timber saw. Then the tree would begin to sway and finally gracefully yield, slowly tipping over. The new cut would give off a distinctive smell, something between turpentine and rosin. A few more strokes with the saw or the double-headed axe and the tree would fall clear, leaving a white, naked stump. When all the designated trees were cut, we would drag them (a la Currier & Ives) to a central point.

Originally, I believe that my father had made deliveries on Christmas Eve. However, this schedule caused universal dismay. No matter how freshly cut, no one wanted the job of setting up a large, ungainly Norway Spruce on Christmas Eve, especially if the hour was late. Thus, by the time my brother and I were old enough to help, deliveries were made on the Saturday or Sunday before Christmas. If it was a Saturday, my father would leave his law office at the usual Saturday 1:00 P.M. closing time. He would pick up my brother and me. In high spirits, we would then drive out into the country and borrow Levi Hollingsworth's truck and drive it back over to our Centerville property. Once there, the three of us would pile a great load of trees on the truck and rope them down with great gordian knots. That done, we would set out on our first round of deliveries. Typically, we would draw up to a house and stop. We would then clamber all over the load of trees in order to find the tagged tree in question, undo the knots and wiggle the chosen tree out of the pile. The tree would then be dragged up onto the lawn or onto the porch. That done, we would bang on the door. The lucky recipient would come out and duly admire the great bushy tree with a jagged stump that stood on the porch, obscuring the front door. As noted, our basic problem always was that our Norway spruce grew so quickly and so sturdily that, all too often, the tree in question was a tad larger, even in our own view, than what might be called for by the fragile living room for which it was destined. Nevertheless, in the spirit of Christmas, these huge green trees appear to have been gratefully received, or at least we thought so. We, of course, were in the roughest of working clothes, since the cutting and delivering of Christmas trees was dirty work at best. We would be welcomed into the house and duly issued Christmas cheer, which as we boys got older, got stronger.

Since we had deliveries to make literally all over New Castle County, the task went on well into the evening. Indeed, in the middle of our round of deliveries, we would stop off at our house, ravenously hungry, and demand an immediate supper so we could get back to our Noël rounds. After a hasty supper, we would pile back aboard the truck for yet another jovial round of deliveries. It was usually well past midnight when our Christmas task was done. We would redeliver the truck to Levi Hollingsworth's shed. Then we would stand for a while in the moonlight or starlight and enjoy the night, the country, and the festive rounds that we had just completed. It was great good fun.

However, my mother who was Gallic by origin, was not amused at all by these annual Christmas tree shenanigans. First, Christmas trees were Germanic in origin. Second, she, for some reason, did not fancy being left all alone, orginally on Christmas Eve or years later on the Saturday or Sunday before Christmas. Finally, it did not amuse her one bit to have her husband and sons stomp in between rounds, loudly demanding dinner and then coming home at all hours, after roistering all night on Christmas cheer. However, annually we disallowed these complaints as not being in keeping with our view of Christmas. We were sure that we were performing a service for the community and the lucky recipients of our huge coniferous offerings.

However, I noticed that my father's list did not grow over the years. On the contrary, it got smaller. At times, we three wondered why people kept removing themselves from the list. When we would call to inquire as to what size tree they wanted on this particular year, all too often they replied that they had already committed to this church or that fire company or that they had bought a tree or were going away or simply would not require a tree from us that year. However, as I think back, there are certain incidents now that stand out in my mind that should have warned us that our heroic and jovial efforts were somewhat overdone.

The first of these episodes involved a lady (who shall remain nameless) who had just had her handsome dining room redone with a tray ceiling. The dining room was the place in the house where the Christmas tree had always stood. Thus, when the front door was opened, I manfully dragged a great tree past her, over the hardwood floors and Persian carpets and on into the dining room where a small ladies' lunch to admire the new ceiling was in progress. The lady, looking agitated and apprehensively at her treasured new ceiling, gently suggested that this particular tree might be just a little bit too tall for the handsome new ceiling. I roughly gauged the height of tree and the height of the ceiling and came to a different conclusion. (Perhaps my judgment on the respective heights might have been a mite affected by the Christmas cheer that I had imbibed at previous houses on this particular round.) Be that as it may, I quickly decided to determine the matter by raising the tree. I swung it up: it turned out that the hostess was right and that I was dead wrong, perhaps by 9 to 12 inches. The bristly top of the freshly cut green tree first bent over against the pure white ceiling, leaving a bright green line across it. But, the worst was yet to come: when I had the tree straight up, the stiff top of the new cut tree popped right on through the treasured new ceiling, putting a great ugly hole in it. There was a ghastly silence all the way around for a full thirty seconds. Then, the lady graciously said that it really didn't make any difference: surely no one would notice the huge hole at all. She added wistfully that, after all, the ceiling could be redone after Chistmas. My father and brother compounded the damage that I had done by pulling the tree back down, again thus enlarging the ugly hole. Need it be said that the lady made it plain that, on several occasions well before the next December rolled around, she would not be needing a tree from us. In fact, she called us on Dcember 10th to say that she had already purchased a table-sized tree which she had placed in the hall and had already decorated.

Then there was the time that we somehow managed to lose our last small tree. We ended up that particular round with nothing other than a 9-foot tree. We could barely force it up the the steps and in the front door of the small apartment of the luckless recipient. She somewhat ruefully said later that she had kept it there all through Christmas though she and her family had not been able to go into the living room at all and that it had cost her a small fortune to have the building superintendent drag this green monster back out again after New Year's. She did add, however, that though the apartment had had a delicious woodsy smell, please to count her out.

Again, I remember that we had been delivering trees for a number of years to an old friend of my father's and his wife. They were always very cordial and very effusive in their praise of the freshness and fullness of our trees. Then, for some inexplicable reason, we totally forgot them one year, believing as we stood in the moonlight after our rounds were completed that we had in fact delivered a tree to them. It was only later that we found out that they had waited in vain for their tree only to have to go out the day before Christmas when Christmas tree prices were at their highest and buy a dingy old Vermont tree that had been cut back in October. These people wisely made their own provisions for dependable Christmas trees in the following years. Thus, they dropped themselves off our dwindling list.

One of our oldest "customers" was my father's friend, Judge John Biggs, and his wife, Anna, a courtesy aunt of mine. Judge Biggs stoutly protested that putting the tree up was a nuisance that inter- fered with the real pleasures of Christmas, nevertheless the Judge and Anna were always affable when we would finally wind our way up their bumpy drive. The late arrival of our truck would rouse their dogs who would bark their heads off. Though they were often in bed or at least ready for bed and reading comfortably, they would put on bathrobes and come down and turn on the outside lights, hush the dogs, and duly admire the large tree that stood propped against their yellow house. Afterwards, we would all troop into the Judge's study. Drinks would be poured and the Judge's precious Cuban cigars would be offered to my brother and me. In an hour or so, we would leave the Judge and Aunty Anna to their Christmas peace. We would bang and rattle our way down their winding graveled drive. On the last occasion of our delivery to them, however, we found that we had again managed to lose a tree. Thus, we had no tree to deliver at our next stop. After a council of war, it was decided that we would go quietly back to the Biggs' and "borrow" the tree that we had given them and give it to the next recipient. Later, we would go back out into our fields and cut another tree, even fresher and bigger, for the Biggs'. Thus all would be well. Indeed, all would have been well, except that the dogs again set up a terrific uproar. The Judge stuck his head out his bedroom window and saw that somebody in the darkness below him was purloining the tree that had just been delivered to him. The Judge summoned the State Police. They stopped us at the covered bridge, demanding to know who these three scruffy people were, why they were driving a truck that didn't belong to them loaded with a Christmas tree that belonged to a United States Circuit Court Judge. In the end, we had to make a third trip back up the hill, arousing the dogs and, of course, again waking the Judge and Aunty Anna. To make a long story short, we eventually did go back in the field and cut another tree. It was delivered at about 3:00 A.M. that morning. Our delivery again roused the dogs and the Judge. That was our "Swan Song" with Judge Biggs and Aunty Anna.

In time, some of my friends had been added to my father's list of those who annually got a Christmas tree. Here again, initially, we were greeted with open arms, but our Noël exuberance and excess brought this gracious custom to an end with my friends. For example, Laird and Peggy Stabler built themselves a handsome house with a magnificent hall and a beautiful curved staircase. It was obvious that the center of the staircase was a place where a tall Christmas tree should go: it would seem to disappear right out of the top of the house. Since, as I say, many of the trees that we had planted over the years had not been cut down and had now grown to truly magnificent height, our efforts for the Stablers became grander and grander. Indeed, Peggy accumulated four closets full of Christmas lights and Christmas ornaments year after year in order to decorate the monsters that we brought her.

The year of our last delivery to the Stablers, there happened to be snow on the ground. Quite apart from our Christmas tree operations, we needed to cut down a huge pine tree that had been there long before my father had started planting Norway spruce. However, it was over-shadowing other trees and Mother had decreed that it must come down. It had grown fully 60 feet high and had a 10-inch base. There-fore, we got out the powersaw and sawed away at the base. With a tremendous crash, this giant pine came down. At the time, we were simply going to chop it up for firewood. Suddenly, we got the idea of delivering it to the Laird Stablers: it would be the granddaddy of all Christmas trees! We therefore got out a large iron chain and fastened it around the butt of this piney Goliath. The other end was hooked to our tractor. We pulled this huge tree on out our drive, down the Kennett Pike through Centerville, over the Center Meeting Road, down Montchanin Road and eventually up the Stablers' drive. The tree was so big that it covered the entire road and no cars could go by. This monster, as it went up the Stablers' drive, knocked down the neat snow stakes on both sides, brushed their own newly planted trees and scattered their white painted rocks. Nevertheless, we persisted on our course of Christmas madness and dragged it right up to the very front door of the house. Fortunately, there was no one at home except a Labrador and a Chesapeake Bay who barked loudly to see "Birnam Wood be come to Dunsinane." Delighted with ourselves, we left the tree in front of the house. The branches at the butt end came up to the second story windows. The prone tree stretched the entire length of the house. Neither the White House, Pennsylvania Station, nor Rockefeller Center had a finer, fresher, or bigger Christmas tree that year than the Stablers. However, this last effort broke the Christmas camel's back. Peg Stabler put her foot firmly down and decreed that reason must return to Christmas. She would not have a Christmas tree that made herself and all of her family look like Liliputians. Thus, we had outdone ourselves at the Stablers, and yet another recipient lopped themselves off our list.

By the end of my father's lifetime his list had dwindled greatly. In spite of the foregoing incidents and indeed many others, he could not understand why his Christmas largesse was not gladly accepted each year by those lucky persons on his list. Those who would still accept a freshly cut Norway spruce were just a small group of the fifty or so that we had delivered to in our heyday, or heynights. After his death, our custom of delivering home grown trees died out entirely: it is a thing of the past.

Now, Christmas has become far more commercial than it was when I was a boy and young man growing up. Fireproof Christmas trees are made of plastic. They can be taken apart and stored in the attic, to be used year after year. They have no pine smell at all. Christmas doesn't begin on some windblown day in March with the planting of a row of small Norway spruce along a wood line. Rather, it starts when *The Wall Street Journal,* around Labor Day, runs a series of articles containing sombre predictions of whether Christmas will be a retail success or not, depending on whether there is a 3% or 4½% increase of sales of Cabbage Patch Dolls over the last year. Christmas Day itself culminates in a deafening cacophony of Christmas carols on the radio. The television screen celebrates the birth of our Savior in a manger in Bethlehem with Christmas specials done by Hollywood celebrities. In retrospect, I fully understand why our customer list fell away. Still, I think that there was something wonderful and special, at least from our point of view, in our quaint custom of growing and delivering our own homegrown trees. I miss it every year at Christmas time, especially the time when all the trees had been delivered and we stood in the crisp December coldness looking up at the stars, the smell of the cut trees still on our clothes.

Thus, as I look back at my catalogue of evergreen trees from western Maine, I fill out an order for two dozen Norway spruce. This year, they will arrive as always in March or April. I will plant them as a sentimental gesture and a reminiscence of Christmas long ago. However, perhaps Annie, my daughter, age eight, will join me as she gets a bit older and we will again deliver Christmas trees to friends, relatives, and neighbors.

# Golf with Father

When I was growing up my father was far too busy recuperating from the ravages of the depression to take the time to indulge in the usual suburban sports that occupied so much of the time of his contemporaries. Actually, until the fateful day around which this narrative centers, I never saw him swing a golf club. However, in the closet under the stairs of the old Victorian house on Delaware Avenue, there were two monstrous leather bags containing an array of old wooden clubs, one of which I knew belonged to him and one of which had belonged to my grandfather, Judge William Prickett. Grandfather had been an avid golfer. Somewhere in a bureau drawer, there is a family photo album containing several old brown photographs of Grandfather and his golfing companions on the links dressed in Edwardian golfing attire with toothy Teddy Roosevelt smiles and walrus mustaches. Indeed, Grandfather was the Club champion. In the trophy cases of the Wilmington Country Club, there are, I believe, still several brass and Sheffield cups commemorating forever his Sunday afternoon victories between 1887 and 1913. I knew my father had caddied in his youth for his father and had played some, but, as I say, I was an utter stranger to the links in my youth and never learned the art of driving, pitching, or putting. However, when I was wasting my time and the taxpayers' money down in Camp LeJeune as a Second Lieutenant during the Korean War, I found out one day that there was a golf course manicured by an army of privates (oh, the good old days!!) for the exclusive use of officers and their wives. Having nothing much to do on weekends in that godforsaken area of the world, I decided to make an effort to learn golf. My efforts met with a dismal lack of success stemming from a lack of coordination coupled with impatience at the repeated necessity, not of animal energy, but of accuracy and control. Indeed, my budding career as the U.S. Marine Corps' answer to Arnold Palmer came to an abrupt end one day when, in a fit of sudden anger at the unpredictable course of the white ball, I took an innocent nine-iron and bent it double by hitting it full force against a nearby and equally innocent swamp maple sapling. When the fat Staff Sergeant in charge of the links saw what I had done to the borrowed nine-iron, he reported me to the Chairman of the Golfing Committee. I got a stern military reprimand from a Colonel whose only duty seemed to be perfecting his golfing technique.

Well, that particular war having come to an end, I returned to civilian life and eventually the practice of law with my father. One day, I idly complained that I had never been taught in my youth any of the suburban sports that so many of my contemporaries were now playing with ease and proficiency. My father decided at that point that golf was a social amenity that should now be added to my pitiful bag of social graces. (As a matter of fact, having seen me stumbling about at a Country Club dance, my father sent me off to take an Arthur Murray dance course to improve my ballroom style. This led to a brief fling with a bosomy Arthur Murray instructress. However, when I took this somewhat voluptuous lady to the next Country Club dance, my father quickly terminated his financial support of that venture. With no financial support, my temptress was no longer interested. Thus, my dancing style has not improved. However, that is another story.)

Back to golf. My father, having decided on a course of action, was not apt to let time go by: he therefore suggested the very next day that we go out on Saturday to the links of the Wilmington Country Club. He and I were members and had supported the regular golfing fraternity by paying the monstrous club dues for years. I was mildly agreeable to the project but pointed out that we did not have any clubs. My father briskly brushed this objection aside, pointing out that he still had his clubs and I could use my grandfather's clubs. I did not know much about golf but did know enough to know that those long wooden relics were not only brittle but were museum pieces rather than effective shiny metal instruments then in use. "Nonsense!", my father replied, "The material out of which the clubs are made is apt to change from time to time, but the form of the clubs has not changed at all since the game was invented back in Scotland centuries ago." He went down and got out the old golf bags, brushed off the cobwebs, blew away the dust, and wiped away the mildew that had grown up on the leather over the years. Then, to his delight, he found six old, scarred golf balls in the dry-rotted pouch on one of the bags. As he pulled out the irons, he remarked, "I am probably as rusty as these old clubs but my form will soon come back. When I used to play," he went on, "it was my goal to make a hole-in-one, but I always just missed."

Thus equipped, we arrived at 2:00 o'clock on a hot Saturday afternoon in July. It took us a considerable amount of time to find the golf pro's shop. Once there, Father announced to the old Scotch pro, Alex Tate, and the assembled caddies, that he and I were going to play a round of nine holes. Mr. Tate tactfully suggested that perhaps I might want to commence by taking a few practice drives or perhaps putting a bit. My father rejected this well-meant suggestion out-of-hand and said that I would surely get the feel of the game as we went along. There were incredulous stares by the caddies at the sight of our ancient golfing weaponry and perhaps even a smile which instantly vanished at the stern look of Mr. Tate: he ruled his caddies with an iron hand and allowed no disrespect to members. Mr. Tate politely asked us if we wanted to use a caddy. Again, my father disdained the proffer, pointing out that the purpose of the game was exercise, and that he and I could easily manage the huge old leather bags. Though I now know that play on Saturdays requires not only a reservation but a foursome, Mr. Tate sized this twosome up as special and quickly pointed out the first tee to us, shouldering aside a serious foursome of fourteen-year old boys who were already proficient golfers.

My father saw no reason not to profit from this outing to get some sunburn. He therefore removed his shirt as we got to the first tee. His outfit consisted of knee length khaki shorts, an old Bermuda straw hat and some walking boots. Of course, in view of his back injury in a plane crash in France in 1917, he wore a back brace. For my part, I was wearing faded Marine greens and a fatigue cap. Though I knew my father had not played for fully forty years, I knew that he never forgot any skill he ever acquired. I was sure that he would perform credibly. However, I had real reservations about how I would fare, especially with his forceful coaching. However, nothing ventured, nothing gained. On this note we set out.

My father first gave me a few pointers. He then hauled out his driver and stepped boldly up to a borrowed tee, having planted one of our precious six old golf balls on a tee. He took a vigorous swing at the ball. He hit the ball and it sailed one hundred yards squarely down the middle of the fairway and came to rest. My father motioned me to tee off. I managed to hit the ball on my first swing but I must have hit it with the side of the club. The ball sort of sailed up in a kind of lazy boomerang course and then came winging back down and came to rest almost at my feet. I could already see that I was not going to burn up any course records, nor indeed was I going to add any glory on my grandfather's record. Indeed, I sensed another golfing disaster in the offing.

My father, sensing my mood, bravely pointed out that golf was a game that took a bit of persistence. He went on to assure me that by the third or fourth hole, if I paid attention, I should soon get the hang of the game. Well, we set out under the blazing hot sun, each carrying our eighty-pound golf bags. I think that I managed to put my replacement golf ball in the first hole after fourteen or fifteen erratic shots. I say "replacement ball" because I lost three golf balls on the first hole. Indeed, I took the precaution of going all the way back to the golf-master's house and purchasing another six white pellets because I could see at the rate I was going, we were not going to even get midway in our round: we would surely run out of the necessary white ammunition to continue the fight. Since these replacement golf balls cost $2.66 apiece, my father cautioned me to be prudent since he didn't want to run up the cost of this expedition by an inordinate expenditure on golf balls.

Time has softened the memory of all of the details of the disastrous round that we played. I do remember that the fourteen-year-old four-some, whom we had brusquely shouldered aside at the outset, came up behind us not long after we started. They were reasonably patient for two holes but then had the temerity to ask if they might play through. My father at first saw little reason to agree, but in the end he did agree. They did play efficiently through. In a short time, they disappeared over the golfing horizon while I ineffectually batted my ball back and forth cris-cross across the fairways and the greens, only to end up inevitably in the tentacles of the huge sand traps that surrounded the small hole that was the object of my endeavors.

Not long after that, when I had finally "holed" my ball, we walked over to another tee and got ready to tee up for our next drive. All the while, my father was busy giving me a running critique of my form and instructions on what to do and what not to do. We could see the flag but, oddly enough, our drives would have to go over or right through some fairly thick woods that lay between the tee and this particular flag. There was an arm waving and shouting from some other golfers some distance away. However, my father disregarded all this commotion and drove and I followed. To our great surprise, as I was getting ready for my fourth shot and my father's second shot, a golf ball bounded down between us and lay there. We looked at each other in astonishment. Then, we saw four ladies with caddies bearing down on us on what was obviously a collision course with our line of play. My father remarked that the ladies were obviously "off course." The ladies were young matrons. They were very polite to this now lobster-red older man wearing a back brace. They asked politely just where we were going. We pointed to a flag up ahead in the distance. They looked somewhat puzzled in the general direction from which we had just come but neither they nor their caddies said anything but simply swept on by.

It was only when we got closer to the flag itself that we noticed we were approaching the hole from a side that had no sandtraps. Suddenly it dawned on us that perhaps the ladies and the arm wavers had been right after all. Indeed, it turned out that at the last hole, we had teed off in the wrong direction and we had driven towards a pin that actually was on the second nine and across two other fairways. This accounted for the trees that we had had to play through. It also accounted for the fact that we had not encountered the usual sandtraps that had consumed so many of my fruitless strokes; strokes that had made it look like there had been a dog digging or a giant sand-moving operation going on when I was trying to get out. However, even though we recognized now that we were somewhat off course, so to speak, my father decided that we should gamely play the hole out as sportsmen should. There was a total confusion when, as I was completing my seventh putt, we were bombarded with accurately driven second shots that bounced smartly onto the green from the right direction. Indeed, my father was hit by one of these balls in the back, fortunately on its second bounce. It cause him to mis-putt. He was momentarily angry, indicating that courtesy called for the time honored call of "fore." I pointed out to him that the golfers shooting for this pin obviously couldn't see us and had little reason to expect that somebody would be coming from the wrong side. My father agreed that I probably had a good legal point though he said that "fore" was simply a common precaution and courtesy. The golfers in question turned out to be a serious Saturday afternoon foursome who were probably betting a fair amount on each hole. They came storming up, sizzling mad. However, they tempered their threatening looks when they saw my father since they knew that in arguments, my father would take second best from no man. In the end, after our explanation, they gravely said that they could quite understand how this interesting situation had arisen and concluded that they were delighted to see that the son and grandson of a Club champion were coming back to re-establish our family's prowess on the golf links. The caddies, however, out from under the stern eye of Mr. Tate, were openly amused.

It was, however, the seventh or perhaps the eighth hole that is stamped forever in my memory. It was a water hole. The tee sat well above the hole and the water lay in between. The designer of the course had shrewdly posed a tactical problem to the golfer as to whether to drive the ball cleanly over the water and onto the fairway just short of the green, or whether more prudently to take a short tap to this side of the water and then on the second stroke lift the ball over the pond and so to the green. I was undecided as to how to play this obstacle. We, at this point, had only two remaining balls. Obviously, if the water gobbled up our two balls, our play would be finished. We would be forced to march back in without having completed the nine. As I teed up, my father suggested that this was the sort of hole on which my grandfather had made several "holes-in-one." He said that if I would only follow his instructions, I ought to be able to put the ball on the green, if not in the hole with one stroke. Of course, these well-meant reminders of ancestral prowess and techniques did nothing for my coordination or self-confidence. The result was reflected in my faltering stroke. I took careful but shaky aim at the ball with my five-iron. I must have again hit under the ball. It flew skyward and was lost to our upward gaze in the penetrating rays of the July sun. We both put our hands over our heads to avoid being pelted by my skyward shot in case of another "boomerang." However, the boomerang effect was not built into this shot. Instead, the ball came whistling down out of the clouds and splashed into the pond, raising a great cascade of water. My father immediately took a careful sight on the ball and suggested that I not tempt the fates by exposing our one remaining golf ball to a watery grave. Rather, I should go down and retrieve the ball. Well, down we went and stood on the edge on the pond. My father, who was an ex-artillery man, roughly triangulated the spot where the ball must be at rest on the muddy bottom of the pond. Other golfers had come up and were now waiting somewhat impatiently. They watched in wonderment as my father did his sightings with a golf club and then made some rough calculations. He said that the ball could not be more than seven feet in from the edge. I pointed out that the pond was stagnant and had a soft bottom. But he replied, "Nonsense, that should be nothing for an old Marine!" After further parental advice about not wasting money on lost golf balls, to the amazement of those behind us, I waded into the greenish waters of the pond. The golf ball had obviously sunk into the eighteen inches of soft gray alluvial mud. It will remain there for time immemorial (or until such time as some future archeologist pulls it out. I wonder what scientific explanation will be given by such a digger who will recover so many of these small, white rubber balls that our generation will seem to have planted with so much pain in particular ponds about the country-side.)

Well, I spent a good ten minutes searching around for the ball while the Saturday afternoon golfers piled up. In the end, there was quite a crowd watching this aquatic maneuver for one lost golf ball. Finally, as the crowd on the tee began to murmur angrily, my father called me out. I was covered with mud and had to bathe to get the mud off. I then shook myself like a wet Lab or Retriever. I rejoined my father on the bank. Then my father turned and marched boldly back up the hill to the tee. Firmly overruling the protests of the waiting legions of golfers, he teed up our last scarred old golf ball. He then took his rusty five-iron, addressed the ball and gave it a smart blow. The ball sailed cleanly over the pond and bounced onto the green. The ball seemed to have a mind of its own: it rolled aimlessly around the green for a while. Then, seeming to make up its mind, it rolled over to the cup and dropped in. There was a stupefied moment of silence during which my father went and calmly picked up his borrowed tee. Cheers and exclamations erupted from the erstwhile angry crowd to my father's genuine astonishment.

Then, father joined me saying that we had had a good day and that we were making a good beginning on my golfing game. When we got back to the golf shop, Mr. Tate suggested that we leave the antiquated clubs there and that he could perhaps get some of the rust off and refurbish the bag in case I took up my father's offer to get a few lessons and really take the game up.

So far as I know, the golf bag is still there. Perhaps it has found its way into the archives of the Club or some museum. However, certain it is that I never went back to the golf greens again. My father never played again. He ended up with a monstrously stiff back. Besides, he had achieved his golfing goal: a hole-in-one!

# Wolfgang Amadeus Prickett

When I tell my daughter Annie, age 9, to do something, there is always a little flicker in her eyes before she does as I say. I know full well that she is deciding each time whether she will or she won't do as I say. She mentally calculates each time whether she can defy me, get around me, or wear me down, or pull off a "trifecta," a combination of all three. It was far different, however, in the good old days when I was growing up in the 1930s. There was never any question whatsoever when my father told me to do something as to whether or not I was going to do it. In other words, when my father said "jump," no matter how gently, it was not a question of whether I would or would not jump: the question was "how high" and "how often." Times have changed: parental authority is not what it used to be.

However, when I came back after a stint in the U.S. Navy during World War II, my father quickly recognized that having marched to orders other than his, his orders to me probably were not going to be followed with alacrity any more. He knew that he had better not say "jump," expecting me to defy the laws of gravity again. However, as this little tale shows, my father had other weapons in his parental quiver to achieve any objective that he thought desirable if he could no longer attain such objective by a simple direct command.

Now this story starts with a fundamental premise—that is, that I am not and never was a musician. Indeed, the first report from the progressive education school where I spent my early years was discouraging about many things including my musical ability (or rather my total lack of musical ability to put it more accurately). Indeed, as to music, the report stated bluntly: "Your Bill is an enthusiastic and clumsy child. He has no eye to hand coordination and no ear or rhythm. He likes to shout more than he likes to sing." (I am sure some of my colleagues will say this report is still true.) I must say that over the years my ability to make music did not improve much, though living in my father's and mother's household, I was exposed to reams of classical music and came in time to not only enjoy it but enjoy it immensely.

On the other hand, my father was an amateur musician. For example, he had gotten into the Triangle Club at Princeton by playing the violin. My mother was a passable musician, as all young women of her era were—that is, she could play something on the piano and had studied the violin. She had played a reluctant viola when my father enthusiastically promoted a string quartet in the 20s. My sister had dutifully taken up the piano. However, when I was eight years old or so, it was universally decided that I was a musical lout and not trainable. Hence, I was able to avoid the tedium of endless piano lessons and enforced practice that were my sister's lot in life before she went off to boarding school and Smith College.

When I came back to Delaware after having served in the U.S. Navy during the closing days of World War II, it was assumed that after the summer, I would go back to Princeton again. (I had been accepted to Princeton before going off to serve in the fleet. Princeton recognized that it would have to make good on its wartime undertakings even though it was now overwehelmed with a rash of discharged veterans, many of whom had far better credentials and indeed higher aims than I did). My father rejoiced in my undeserved good luck in being able to go back into a university far above my intellectual gifts or my propensity for work of any kind. I knew privately, however, that I was well-fitted for Princeton University, having trained extensively in the taverns and inns that cater to the Navy. But I was not at all sure that I really wanted to plunge back into the rarified atmosphere of such a university.

One day after I came home from the Navy, I sat down at Mother's piano. I played around with the keys, not having much else to do. Eventually, I came up with a little six bar air that had a classical sound as opposed to jazz or rock (or as opposed to nothing, which is what it was). It was hard to say whether it was more like Bach or Brahms, Schumann or Schubert, but it sounded classical all the same. People around the house said it was nice. Mother's friends looked up from between stout drinks at their rubbers of bridge and remarked on what a really fine piece of music the six bars were. One lady said that it was perfect Chopin. Another, downing her third rye and soda, and before getting another, said that it sounded like early Tchaikovsky. The third lady who was non-musical, said that she didn't know what it was but she liked it all the same. Mother said nothing: she knew musical garbage when she heard it. However, the damage had been done. The seed had been planted in my brain that I was a musical genius. I went on playing my little air over and over again. Even the dogs got sick of it. They would whine to be let out of the house whenever I sat down at the piano. However, I knew that they were a non-musical group of mutts.

One summer day at breakfast while we were living at the summer house in Centerville and I was feeling a trifle surly from too many beers the night before, my father said brightly that he supposed that I would be going back to Princeton in the fall. To my father's utter surprise, I said flatly, "No, as a matter of fact, I am not going back to Princeton at all." I told my astonished father, mother, brother, and sister that in fact, I had decided that I would take up music and become a composer. My father looked dumbfounded. Then he began scratching the hair in back of his left ear, a gesture that he always unconsciously did when he was cross, annoyed, or very angry. That gesture reinforced my new found musical determination.

However, my father very quickly got himself under control. He said nothing more at the time.

The next day at breakfast, I expected to receive a paternal lecture on the value of a college education and what a fine college Princeton was. However, I was determined that I wasn't going to jump just because my father said so. My father looked benignly around the table and then quietly announced: "I thought Bill was going back to Princeton but he has now decided to become a musician." My sister Elise giggled but my father shushed her up with a stern look. My father continued, "I was a musician in my youth. Indeed, it was my ability to play the violin that got me into the Princeton Triangle Club. I think that it is fine that one of my children has decided to become a musical composer." My mother's eyes opened slightly. A look of Gallic disbelief crossed her face but she said nothing: she knew that my father was going to take care of this little musical escapade all in his own way and time. She knew better than to interfere. I must say that I felt slightly incredulous but managed to look around and smile. My father went on: "Now my other son will graduate from Princeton if he keeps his nose to the grindstone. But Bill here will become a composer.

"Now the first thing that I'm going to do for Bill is to get him the basic skills that he will need including the ability to play the piano." My father went on to spell it out.

My father's plan was simple and straightforward. It was all that I could possibly have demanded in my wildest artistic dreams (and dreams they were). We had a big Victorian house next to the Soldiers' and Sailors' Monument at 1401 Delaware Avenue, which my father had inherited from his father. We lived in a summer house in Centerville, Delaware. The town house was always closed up for the summer. Dust covers were placed all over the furniture. The rugs were rolled up. The venetian blinds and curtains were drawn and tightly closed. It was as still as an Egyptian tomb in this musty old Victorian house. Each year it had to be aired out completely in early September when we moved back into town again just before school started. It is still there if you care to see it, shorn of its Victorian finery and now divided into several handsome apartments and doctors' offices. (It does not as yet have a bronze plaque announcing that this was the first practice studio of Wolfgang Amadeus Prickett).

My father pointed out that there was a big Baldwin grand piano in the main living room. Indeed, its action was rather like that of a Baldwin steam locomotive. My father said that I could accompany him and go to the town house in the morning. I would have the house all to myself. I could practice to my heart's content without the annoyance of a younger brother, a nearby swimming pool and all the other distractions that might take an otherwise giddy young composer away from the business of learning music. After two hours of practice, I could then take the streetcar and go across the Brandywine out on Baynard Boulevard where Ms. Osborne, a retired teacher from the Wilmington Music School, gave private piano lessons to gifted students. She would give me an hour of instruction on the piano and an hour on musical theory. Then I would catch the streetcar back to the Victorian house to have a sandwich lunch from a brown paper bag. I was then free to spend the entire afternoon practicing the piano. My father would pick me up at 6:00 P.M. and bring me to Centerville. After dinner, I could practice at home on the somewhat smaller piano in the country house or I could spend the time until bedtime listening to old classical records on the wind-up Victrola. Once I had gotten the basics down, then Juilliard, Nadia Boulanger, the Elizabeth Competition, and on to Moscow!

I was speechless. My stern old father had given way. I was to have my way. And it happened just the way my father said it would. I went on into town the first day and my father dropped me off at 1401 Delaware Avenue. The first day worked just fine. I spent the day at the house practicing my little air and experimenting with the piano. I had rather enjoyed taking the trolley across the Brandywine and up to Ms. Osborne's house. However. Ms. Osborne turned out to have a couple of nasty features. She was an older, prim sort of lady with steel rimmed glasses and a no-nonsense attitude towards music lessons. She had the nasty habit of wacking me smartly across the fingers with a rule when I goofed off or hit a wrong note. This happened quite often and it hurt.

Furthermore, as we bent over scores learning theory, I discovered that she had really bad breath! However, in spite of the foregoing, I thought at first that it was great. I continued to have sort of Walter Mitty visions of conducting my own piano concerto at the Opera House in Vienna or sitting in a box as Toscanini bowed to me at the conclusion of a great artistic triumph of mine.

The second day was pretty much like the first day except that it began to get just a trifle boring in the big Victorian house at the end of the day. The third day I was really bored. I had come to share the dogs' view of my little air. I was tempted to duck Ms. Osborne's lessons on the fourth day.

Well there is no use stringing this out any longer. I lasted, I think, a week or maybe eight days. At the end of that time, I began begging off. By the end of two weeks, my father had reclosed the town house and had paid Ms. Osborne off. Actually, as I think back on it I am sure that she was in league with him from the start. She may well have applied the ruler a little bit more frequently and with more vigor than she would have done with any other clumsy young man. After all, she could tell a Mozart from a sow's ear. Clearly, the young man that she had under instruction was not a second Wolfgang Amadeus.

I returned to Princeton in the fall totally cured of my musical ambitions and dreams—they have never recurred.

My father had handled a difficult situation with skill and affection.

# Flunking the Bar

This painful account is really only addressed to one small group of unfortunate people: those, who, like the writer, have had the truly awful experience of flunking a Bar Exam. I write this account, not only to air an ancient wound, but to share the common misery of what happened with others who, like myself, coming bright and shiny out of law school, have failed the ultimate professional hurdle that allows them to represent clients before the Courts. Those who have not suffered such a professional humiliation should read no further, unless in reading about my downfall, the reader would get the almost obscene pleasure in gloating over the deserved comeuppance of a snotty young ivy leaguer and a graduate of the Harvard Law School—or unless an account of long-awaited retribution of a crusty old Delaware Bar Examiner is something that you can truly savor.

If my caveat and disclaimer have been disregarded, let us proceed with this melancholy tale, for melancholy it still is for me and all others who have come a cropper at the very threshold of their legal careers.

This account must start with my late father—the crusty Delaware Bar Examiner. On his return from World War I in 1919, he did not have to take the Delaware Bar Examination. Not only was he a decorated and injured World War I artillery officer and flyer, but he had come back to Wilmington armed with a war bride, my mother, from poor, little, ravaged Belgium. In addition, he, I believe, was the only person applying for admission to the Delaware Bar that year. Thus, I believe that the nine senior lawyers who constituted the Delaware Board of Bar Examiners considered his war record and his brief attendance as a Rhodes Scholar at Oxford and decided that there was no necessity for making this war hero take the Bar Exam, expecially as his own father was a Delaware lawyer and part-time judge. (Oh, for the good old days!)

It should be said that in those days the complete power to admit or reject would-be lawyers in Delaware, as in most States, was vested in the Delaware Supreme Court. The Court in turn appointed an advisory committee known as the Board of Bar Examiners, which in effect wielded the admitting power for the Court. In olden times, this Board almost automatically consisted of nine senior respectable members of the Bar. The Board looked on its task as one of preserving the right to audience before the Courts to persons whom they themselves found acceptable and congenial (*i.e.,* good old boys—and when I say boys, I mean boys). The Board required those who aspired to become full-fledged Delaware attorneys to be preceptees or clerks to the members of the Bar for six months during or after law school but before being admitted to practice. There were continual and unavailing whispered complaints that the clerkship program was enforced peonage and thus contrary to the Thirteenth Amendment. Of course, no one even contemplated saying anything out loud about the clerkship requirement, much less doing anything about it (such as bringing a class action suit).

In addition, before they could achieve even the threshold status of clerks, each would-be attorney had to appear in front of a panel of the Board of Bar Examiners to be examined by these august attorneys on an ancient tome written in 1921—Zane's *Story of the Law*. Later, I asked my father why it was that the Board continued to use that truly awful book. Zane was not only highly opinionated on the conservative side, but the book was full of the most outrageous historical errors and blunders. I pointed out that Justice Oliver Wendel Holmes had written a fine book entitled *The Common Law* that might provide a basis for a colloquy between the aspiring lawyers and the Board of Bar Examiners.

My father replied that there were several good and sufficient reasons why Zane continued to be used. First, the members of the Board of Bar Examiners were all familiar with Zane, errors and all. It would take considerable time and effort on their part to read and become knowledgeable about another book, especially a "radical" book like Holmes's *Common Law*. Secondly, they knew that the practice of law has many tedious aspects (an understatement if there was one!). Wading through and becoming entirely familiar with Zane would give some indication as to whether the would-be lawyer had the capacity to take on a boring job and do it well. In reply to my general question as to why there should be a preadmission ordeal by Zane, my father said that the Board of Bar Examiners felt strongly that the "right" to audience before the Courts to represent members of the public was not a "right" at all belonging to anyone who simply happened to get through some law school. Rather, admission to the Bar was a sacred privilege that should be accorded only to those who were qualified in every way to take on this weighty fiduciary responsibility. The Board of Bar Examiners felt that if a young man was not qualified by character, morality, or temperament to take on this sort of task, it was better to tell him right at the outset, rather than let him go to law school and then defeat his legal aspirations afterwards (perhaps even after he passed the Bar). That makes a good deal more sense now than it did when I first heard it. (Of course, it is my perspective that has changed: at the time, I thought it was arrant nonsense, though I had the good sense not to say so.)

As I have said, my father was simply waived into the Bar. Thus, he was admitted with very little knowledge of the law and no knowledge whatsoever of the niceties of procedure. Of course, this meant he was without any misconceptions or windy theories taught by legal academics ("Those who can, do; those who can't, teach"). Rather, my father had to learn in the school of hard knocks. However, from the very first, it is a fact that he gave out more knocks than he received. Indeed, my father became known and respected for his prowess in the Byzantine-like intricacies of the Rules of Procedure of the Delaware Courts. I was told and I believe that these ancient rules had remained virtually unchanged from the rules of pleading adopted by the King's Bench in 1709 after the Great Legal Reforms that marked the later years of good Queen Anne. In time, my father was called upon to become one of the nine members of the Board of Bar Examiners. Of course, his assigned topic on which to make up and grade the Bar examination for would-be lawyers was Delaware practice and procedure. In the next ten to fifteen years, there was many a would-be Daniel Webster who was forever relegated to selling shoes or real estate, owing to his inability to field the nice questions my father put to him and the other candidates in matters of legal practice and procedure. My father was concerned (and rightly so) that those who were about to be turned loose on the public as lawyers should know the basic ABCs of practice and procedure in the Delaware Courts. He had precious little interest in legal theories or balanced arguments so dear to those who teach in law schools: rather, he wanted a plain, simple, and above all, correct answer on questons of practice and procedure that would be immediately critical for the legal success or failure of these would-be Solons and, more importantly, for their clients. Thus, he would ask questions as to how many returns of *non est* were required in order to perfect a sheriff's return (two), or what was the only proper response to an affidavit of demand (a reply affidavit). Simple, if you knew the answer, but fatal if you didn't. No careful essay learnedly discussing pros and cons of what the answer might be or should be would or could pass legal muster with my father.

In due course, Delaware moved out of the middle ages of pleading. In fact, in one large bound, Delaware went from the rear of the common law jurisdictions in matters of practice and pleading to the head of the pack. Specifically, Delaware adopted almost verbatim the notice pleading that the Federal Courts had so recently adopted. Thus, the Delaware Rules paralleled the Federal Rules of Civil Procedure, replacing the ancient hoary practices that stemmed back to the time of Blackstone and Coke.

There was a great sigh of relief and general rejoicing in the Delaware legal community at this monumental leap forward. It was also privately hoped that this adoption of entirely new Rules would put my father right square out of business. It was thought that he would be left with a vast storehouse of knowledge of medieval pleadings but would be at a loss when it came to simple, straightforward factual statements of what a case was actually about. However, my father heartily approved of the Rule changes. Further, he put "his money where his mouth was" by chairing the committee that adopted the proposed new Rules for Delaware. My father later told me that he saw no reason why he could not learn the new Rules as quickly as any other Delaware lawyer. He also surmised that he could deal with the merits of a case if he had to as handily as any other Delaware lawyer, be he neophyte or veteran.

That year my father then examined the newest crop of law school graduates on the new Rules of Procedure. They, of course, had had courses on the new Rules at their respective law schools. They felt comfortable in discoursing on all the theoretical problems that might arise under the new Rules. However, my father's bent remained practical: he, for example, would ask that they draft two complaints based on stated facts, one to be filed in the Federal Court and one to be filed in the State Court. There were significant but subtle differences between the Rules in the two Courts. He wanted to make sure that the differences were understood by the applicant because these differences could well spell the difference between victory and defeat for his client. Again, there was wailing and gnashing of teeth, since many who thought they were saved were not among those who passed.

Over the years, my father became known as the toughest of the Board of Bar Examiners. Indeed, at times, his colleagues, not as severe as he was, would overrule his wholesale slaughter of the year's entire crop and admit some aspirants who, he could and would point out, seemed not fully qualified. In due course, however, his term as a member of the Board of Bar Examiners expired. He retired, having amply fulfilled what he had conceived to be his duty to the Supreme Court and to the public.

However, my father's approach had not been entirely draconian. One time, I saw him look up from his nightly task in the fall of correcting the Bar exams. He gave a hearty laugh. He said that the student whose paper he was marking had written a response to one question in some sort of gibberish. He read it to us. My sister remarked brightly that the answer was as plain as the nose on anyone's face: it was written in pig latin.

"Pig Latin! What is that?" my father asked in astonishment. My father's language of choice was Oxford English, albeit with somewhat of a Delaware accent. We three children thereupon spent the rest of the evening talking entirely in pig latin among ourselves to the amusement of my father and consternation of my mother, to whom English remained a second language. The student had written the following answer to this question:

> *State in plain, understandable language how many returns of service are required in an action of detinue.*

His answer in pig latin to the question was something like this as I recall:

> *I ouldway atherway oinjay a ircus and avehay a aintedpay acefay ikelay a lowncay orfay the estray of ymay ifelay if histay is the ortsay of hingtay hatay awyerslay do and hargecay the ublicpay orfa.*\*

My father thought that this showed a daring approach to the problem. To the young man's considerable surprise, he passed procedure. Further, this particular lawyer went on to become an excellent practitioner of law, including procedure. Of course, he owes his professional career to a solid grounding in pig latin.

Thus, my father had become a symbol of the bad old clubby days in terms of admission to the Bar when, having graduated from Harvard Law School, I came back to Wilmington. I, for my part, was as saucy as a jaybird. After all, had I not been to an ivy league college? Had I not successfully graduated from the Harvard Law School? Had not my father and grandfather been respected members of the Delaware Bar? "Pride goeth before a fall and a haughty spirit leads to destruction." Not satisfied with strutting about with all these self-appointed accolades, I compounded my almost certain fate by an incredible series of overbearing acts. First, I plunged into the work at my father's office as if I were already admitted. Further, I did not hesitate to contradict and

---

\* *I would rather join a circus and have a painted face like a clown for the rest of my life if this is the sort of thing that lawyers do and charge the public for.*

correct older admitted lawyers, even though I did not yet have the right to practice. Beyond that, when I ran into my fellow aspirants, I disdained their fearful looks and nervous apprehension about the upcoming Bar examination. It just never occurred to me that anybody with my extraordinary ability and credentials could stumble over something as minor as a provincial Bar Exam. Indeed, I had totally forgotten that a witty professor at Harvard told me, after I had recited poorly in class, to get a treatise by one Milne from the library because the second line on page 37 contained a perfect description of me. He told me to report to the class the next day on what I found. To unending guffaws of my class, I had to report that Milne had said in the words of Christopher Robin: "Oh Pooh Bear, you are a bear of very little brain."

There was a young lady who had studied at a fine, thorough, small law school. She confided to me one day in the law library where I was looking up weighty English precedents that she was very worried about the Bar Exam. She said that she and two young men were holding a study group at nights in order to go over questions that had been given on prior exams and thus preparing themselves for the current Bar Exam. She invited me to attend. (Privately, I told myself that this was simply a crude attempt by the lady to profit by my obvious knowledge and slide into the Bar on my intellectual coattails.) I said somewhat patronizingly that I thought that what they were about was probably a good idea for them, but I was far too busy with the important cases that had been confided to me to take the time to attend any such skull sessions.

In due course, the examination day rolled around. I showed up with all the other candidates. Some of them looked quite gray with fear and apprehension. I was serenely confident as I calmly wrote my assigned number down on the first answer booklet. Some measure of my self-delusion can be gleaned from the fact that never, in the course of the three day examination, did it ever occur to me that I was doing anything other than writing the definitive answers to the questions posed. When the day's examinations were over, there were always huddled conferences in the hallways. Some candidates were concerned that they had missed this issue or that answer. I disdained all such post-mortems and quickly got back to the office to help with the case load. My father, deluded, I suppose, by paternal pride, never questioned that I might not have done what was necessary in preparing for these crucial examinations. Once the examinations were over, I promptly forgot entirely about them and went about my self-important legal business (and pleasures).

Thus, on Saturday, October 16, 1954, I got up and came in town from my digs for a leisurely breakfast at the old Toddle House Diner on Delaware Avenue. Every detail of that painful day is seared into my memory! I remember everything that happened with the garish clarity of last night's nightmare. Thus, I remember that I bought a *Wilmington Morning News*. I scanned it loftily as I waited for my poached eggs. As I was idly turning the pages, an article caught my eye—"The Results of the Delaware State Bar Examination." Ahh, I thought. I looked it over. In the list of those who passed, I could not find my name. I looked back over the list more carefully and still could not find my name. Then hastily, I went through it backwards to see if that produced anything. I noted ominously that the article said that 13 applicants had failed the examination. Pointedly, the article stated that the names of those who had flunked were not published. Suddenly, with the clarity of a flash of lightening, the awful truth dawned on me.

My fork dropped back onto my plate of poached eggs. My hand shook as I tried to take a bracing slurp of black coffee. Unless there had been some awful oversight or error in the marking of the examinations or a mix-up of the assigned numbers, I had failed the Delaware Bar Exam. I telephoned my father. He was, of course, already at the office. I told him what the newspaper revealed. He took it stoically and said something for which I will always be grateful: "Never mind, I still think you have the qualities to make a Delaware lawyer. It just means that you will have to take the Bar Exam again next year."

When I got to the office, my father had already called the Secretary of the Board of Bar Examiners. The Secretary had the difficult task of confirming the fact that I had indeed totally failed the Bar Exam: I had missed, not narrowly, but by a country mile. Worse, the results had been public information the day before. Thus, it was known "on the street" that the son of the feared Bar Examiner of yesteryear had failed. I had walked around in snooty ignorance of the fact that I had just made a total ass of myself. I dumbly wondered how many people I had talked to the day before knew what I had not known—that is, that I had blown the Bar Exam. I wondered if I had compounded this fiasco by some further asinine patronizing statement that had been characteristic of my attitude before that precise moment.

Unfortunately, I had made plans to go to a football game that fall day: I could not back out. I spent a day of acute misery with young friends who were as happy as only young alumni can be at their university for a fall football game and general revelry. I did not want to mar the day by announcing my own intellectual downfall. When asked about the Bar, I had to casually dissemble: already I was trimming sail by saying vaguely that the Delaware Bar Exam was a somewhat dicey matter even for a Harvard Law School graduate.

This justified downfall, however, had several beneficial results. In the first place, it justifiably gave an awful lot of people secret satisfaction at my discomfiture and that of my father: they were fully entitled to savor this retributive moment. Second, it assured any doubters that the Delaware Bar Examination system was fair and impartial. Finally, it taught me a well-deserved lesson in humility and a more realistic evaluation of my own limited gifts.

I spent a sober, modest year working as a clerk in my father's office, not only learning the virtues of modesty and diligence but learning some practical law. I had received a sympathetic phone call from the young lady who had so diffidently inquired as to whether I wanted to join her study group. She, of course, had passed and was a practicing lawyer for a number of years and thus was always my senior at the Bar. She did not even suggest (as I probably would have done) that I had gotten precisely what I had deserved. Instead, she was sympathetic and helpful. Incidentally, she has gone on to higher and better things: she is a successful wife and mother. Remembering her professional solace, I try to make a special effort with colleagues who have stumbled on their initial attempt at the Bar Exam.

When the time rolled around in the spring to begin serious preparations for the Bar Examinations, I not only joined a group but formed one consisting of those that I thought were the ablest young men and ladies who were going to take the Bar Exam that year. I applied myself earnestly to the preparation for the awesome Delaware Bar Examination. When the time came, I sat down with sweaty palms and a butterfly feeling in my stomach.

I spent many sleepless nights between the time of the Bar Exam and the dreaded day when the results were due out. However, the Secretary of the Board of Bar Examiners was kindly disposed towards the now apprehensive father and son. He telephoned us personally just as soon as the Bar results became official that year. I had not only passed but had done well. I almost wept with pleasure at this news. My father was quietly pleased. I must say that there was a spate of felicitations and congratulations from the Bar generally and the Bench. People, after all, were kindly and well-disposed.

There simply could not possibly be a single Delaware lawyer or judge who is not familiar with the seminal Delaware case on the effect and scope of general releases, *Hockem v. Rising Sun Trucking Company,* Del. Supr., 199 A. 2d 1471 (1956). *Hockem* has been cited by the Courts and appears regularly in bar exams in connection with questions about general and special releases. There is no use shepardizing *Hockem* or running it through Lexis. *Hockem* has been repeatedly cited, never questioned and, of course, never overrruled. Serious legal scholars will, of course, check the foregoing assertion, but rest assured that it is correct.

This little story will, however, provide some fresh insight on how that great landmark decision came into being. On the one hand, those who are interested in the law of general releases should consult that scholarly, unanimous opinion by the three great justices who made up the new Supreme Court of Delaware when it was first formed in 1952. On the other hand, those who like to peek behind the judicial curtain (sort of like Dorothy in the Wizard of Oz) and see how such a decision really came to be can read on. Of course, if you do, you should be mindful of Bismarck's remark: "One should neither watch sausage nor the law being made. If one does, one would never, under any circumstances, have anything to do with either one."

This story is titled "May It Please the Court?". It is with this archaic mumbo-jumbo phrase that Delaware lawyers (and indeed lawyers in all English systems of law) commence their legal arguments addressed to Courts. Of course, the phrase is nonsense when one really thinks about it, but so is a good deal of the law and no one ever does really think about such matters. But you will soon discover that my first argument to the Delaware Supreme Court did not please the Court one damn bit, to put it plainly. Nevertheless, I won the *Hockem* case. The result, as is known, was a landmark opinion. The reasons why my oratory did not please the Court are plainly set out, but on the other hand, neither did the arguments of my so-called "worthy friend" (to use another phrase that lawyers since the time of Hogarth and Daumier have mouthed about one another) please the Court. In other words, neither argument pleased the Court, but the Court came up with the definitive opinion on the scope and effect of general releases. How did this come to be?

My first argument before the Supreme Court of Delaware was in about 1956. The Supreme Court of Delaware had only come into being in 1952. At the time of its creation, the Supreme Court consisted of only three justices, but the three persons originally appointed were the most distinguished Delaware lawyers at the time: Chief Justice Clarence Southerland, Justice Daniel Wolcott, and Justice James Tunnell. These lawyers had been specially selected to launch the new Supreme Court, it being agreed that their intellect and energy would enhance the already deservedly high reputation of the Delaware judiciary. I had recently been admitted to the Bar. I had no business whatsoever coming before such an august group of legal scholars. Of course, I was not there by choice. Somehow, I had won a jury verdict for a trucking company against a nasty old school teacher, Miss Hockem. The brakes of the truck owned by the defendant, Rising Sun Trucking Company, had failed and it rear-ended the last in a series of stopped cars. There was a domino effect that rippled all the way right up to the head of the line. In the first car was the nasty old school teacher. The bump, she claimed, gave her a permanent whiplash and aggravated her already testy disposition. However, unfortunately for her, she settled and signed a general release in favor of the driver of the car directly behind her. She then sued Rising Sun and its driver. We pleaded what in "kick the can" used to be called "allee, allee in-free." In the law, that homely phrase describes the principle that a general release releases everyone. The jury, I think, did not like the old school teacher and rather did like our nice truck driver, especially as he was accompanied by a worried, attractive, young, blond woman with three adorable little toddlers. The blond and the infants could have been the defendant's wife and children. In fact, our genial truck driver had just divorced his second wife. The lady was the defendant's sister. The children were neighbors' children whom she was babysitting. Thus, the jury decided against the old harridan and in favor of the cute blond, the toddlers, the genial divorce, the Rising Sun Trucking Company, its insurance company, and, incidentally, me.

An older lawyer, whose name I will have the delicacy not to state, represented the school teacher. In a fit of temper he took an appeal. It was confined to some nice questions on the Byzantine intricacies of general releases. I read it: it was Greek to me. After I had written what I thought was a reasonably presentable answering brief, saying in effect that I had won fair and square in front of a jury of twelve good men and true and that should be the end of the case, I submitted the draft to my father. He was aghast. He spent the next two days and nights reworking the brief to put it in presentable form. From my simple, little effort, the brief grew to a fifty page opus with citations to thirty-three cases and four Law Review articles. I scanned it, but I lost interest halfway through, just about where there was a long discussion of the legal history and meaning of the phrase "but except" running all the way back to Magna Carta. When the brief was filed, my father asked me if I knew how to shepardize cases. (Shepardizing means looking the case up in a publication called Shepard in order to make sure that the case in question has not been overruled or questioned by another Court in a later opinion). I told him that I knew how and would be glad to shepardize the cases in our brief. "Good", said my father, "There are two important cases we rely on that state the minority view which we, of course, need to persuade the Court to adopt. These two particular cases could have been overruled, questioned or limited by later decisions. I do not need to stress the importance of shepardizing these cases, do I?" I replied "Of course not—done!"

My father went on to say that the scope and effect of general releases was a legal subject of abiding interest to him. Thus, he said that if it was all right with me, he would argue the case to the Supreme Court. For my own part, I could take or leave the intricacies of the law of general releases (still can).

Thus, I was just as pleased to leave this highly technical appeal to my father, especially since it appeared to be a matter of professional interest to him and none whatsoever to me. Also, I had no burning desire or indeed any desire at all to appear before the three fearsome justices of the Supreme Court just yet. My father did add that if there was time, he would do a practice argument with me acting as his adversary so I should make myself thoroughly familiar with the briefs, the issues, and the cases. I assured him I would do so and promptly put the argument out of my mind.

My father then looked at my attire. He said that my suit looked as if I had slept in it. (As usual, my father was dead right.) He said that my suits generally not only needed pressing but were apt to be dirty. He told me to get my suit cleaned and pressed before we went to Dover. He also said that I should wear a newly laundered white shirt for the argument. I replied that, at least in my generation, white shirts were thought of as sort of "square." My father, in exasperation, said that that was all very well: perhaps our new Supreme Court consisted of three "squares" but that I should understand that my generation's preference for dirty linen was not the matter in issue: our client's cause was. He said the Supreme Court preferred to have officers of the Court in fresh white shirts rather than looking like roofers after a rough day.

I then went about my own legal business and indeed my pleasure. I did manage to remember to shepardize the cases as instructed except for the two most important ones: the pages referring to these cases were missing. I had meant to go around to the DuPont Company library to finish the job but just had not gotten around to this last little detail. I also fully intended to scan the plaintiff's reply brief.

In due course, the Monday morning rolled around on which the argument was scheduled. I had had a tumultuous weekend culminating in a party most of Sunday night and the predawn part of Monday morning. Thus, I came to the office at 8:30 A.M. with a sort of a dry taste in my mouth and a crashing headache. However, I was young and knew that with a couple of jolts of strong, black coffee and an alka seltser or an aspirin or two, I would probably be right as rain by noon. I had quite forgotten that this was the day that I was to accompany my father to Dover for the argument in *Hockem*. Thus, my suit that particular day was definitely rumpled and not a little soiled.

My father's secretary, Eva Ryan, was waiting for me with a grave look on her face: my father had telephoned her Sunday night: he had had a sudden attack of what he referred to as "lumbago." (Actually, it was a pinched nerve in his back as a result of an airplane crash during World War I.) When it happened my father was totally incapacitated and writhed in his bed until the pain subsided.

I replied to her that I guess that meant that the *Hockem* argument would have to be continued. She smiled grimly and said: "Your father wants to speak to you." I gulped quite audibly (maybe it was a frightened burp).

I telephoned my father. I could tell from his tone that he was indeed in great pain and had taken the rather strong pain killers that he needed when these attacks came on. He told me flatly that I was to handle the argument in *Hockem*. I remonstrated briefly. He replied sternly that I had tried the case and written the answering brief on appeal, or at least the first draft. He assured me I could and should do the argument. However, he admonished me to leave immediately for Dover so as not to take any chances on being late. He then gravely wished me good luck in my first Supreme Court argument and hung up. Just why my father thought I could handle the argument, I still do not know but paternal pride at times interferes with objective judgment. Perhaps it was the pain killers.

Thus, my father, on whom I depended so much at this stage in my career, was totally incapacitated by his recurrent back injury. I felt very lonely indeed as I hung up and faced the grim reality of having to handle entirely on my own a serious appeal which I had not really considered at all.

As I said, when I came into the office, I had quite forgotten the *Hockem* argument. Thus, I did not have a clean, starched, white shirt on at all: rather, I had had a somewhat tired blue Oxford buttoned-down shirt that had withstood the rigors of my vigorous weekend. My first task, therefore, was to run up to Mansure & Prettyman in the DuPont Building as fast as my legs would carry me and buy a white shirt right off the rack. The fussy old clerk simply could not understand why I did not want to discuss the niceties of haberdashery but simply wanted to buy and put on the first white buttoned-down that was my size as soon as I could pull out the hundreds of pins that the shirtmaker had for some reason put in. I was visibly annoyed as his shaky fingers slowly wrote out a spidery sales slip. Then he started to launch into what promised to be a lengthy discourse on my grandfather's preference for starched, detachable, white collars that were in fashion prior to World War I. I left him, his mouth open, quite in the midst of his rambling reminiscences, saying that I was due in the Supreme Court in Dover in fifty minutes, as indeed I was.

I thought, as I raced back to the office to pick up my old car, that I would have time on the way down to Dover to collect my wits. I had a twinge of fright as I remembered that I had not followed my father's admonition that I shepardize all the cases and that I had not read the plaintiff's reply brief at all, much less carefully since my father had not been able to schedule a practice argument. Perhaps I could read the plaintiff's reply brief as I drove down to Dover. My problems were compounded when the claims manager for the insurance company covering the trucking company breezed into our office. He said that he had decided to accompany my father to Dover for the argument. I told him that my father was laid up: I was going to make the argument. He did a massive unconcealed double take, but it was altogether too late to do anything. Thus, we went on off together in my car. As I say, I had hoped that I would have time in the drive down to Dover to assemble my thoughts and prepare a brilliant oral argument. Just why I imagined that I could put anything together that would be even faintly of assistance to the Supreme Court in deciding this case while driving down in excess of the speed limit, now baffles me. However, now having heard a good many arguments, I think that some of my brethren at the bar still believe that the reason the Delaware Supreme Court sits in Dover is to give certain Wilmington and New York lawyers the time to prepare their thoughts and speeches.

As I said, I had the insurance company claims manager with me. He was a frustrated lawyer: he liked nothing better than to wrestle with intricate legal problems. Thus, he at least had read all the briefs. He tried to engage me in a learned discussion on the niceties of the legal points and cases. Of course, he had an advantage or two over me. First, I was desperately hung over. Second, I had only a nodding acquaintance with the plaintiff's opening brief and our answering brief and no acquaintance at all with the reply brief of our opponent. I tried to drive, pay attention to his questions, and nurse my hangover. It was a juggling act that was compounded by the fact that we were going well in excess of the speed limit, mindful of my father's exhortation that under no circumstances should I be late. At one point, I was forced to tell my passenger that, while I was of course fully prepared to make the argument, I had been out a bit later than I would have if I had known my father was not going to make the argument. One thing led to another and I was forced to admit I was slightly hung over (a gross understatement).

My passenger reached in his briefcase, pulled out a pint bottle of Schenley's blended whiskey and unscrewed the cap. The last thing in the world I needed at that point was a belt of hot blended whiskey. But my passenger insisted and, after all, an attorney must do his client's bidding. I gagged down a mouthful. He followed my forced example by taking a triple swig, remarking jovially that it was just the thing "to get the old engine going."

We drew up at the beautiful Green in the center of Dover. Miraculously, I found a parking place. We walked across the Green at a brisk pace and arrived at the awe-inspiring Courtroom at two minutes of 10:00. I was afraid that the first argument might have been continued for some reason and that I would be up to the judicial plate rather than being "on deck," so to speak. That did not happen. At the stroke of 10:00, the bell in the adjoining Courthouse tower began to toll lugubriously. A small door opened and the three justices solemnly and majestically padded toward their chairs. They stood while the clerk solemnly intoned the usual opening concluding with: "God save this honorable Court: all those wishing to be heard may now draw nigh and they shall be heard." As I mentioned, there was another case before ours. Unfortunately, a lawyer (whose name shall remain unstated, at least in this little account) was not present as the Justices sat down. The Chief Justice looked up over his glasses. Then, he asked the missing lawyer's opponent if he knew where his colleague was. The response was in the negative. The Chief Justice then told the Clerk, Jack Messick, to get on the phone to the defendant attorney's office and determine just where this luckless lawyer might be. In the meanwhile, the members of the Court sat, reading the stacks of briefs before them and quietly discussing some of the points of law amongst themselves. In about five minutes, Jack came back. He said that the attorney's secretary had said that the attorney had been delayed in leaving his office and had only left for Dover about 9:25. However, the secretary added that her boss was a fast driver and thus he should be at the Supreme Court "in a jiffy." At just about that time, the lawyer in question came barging into the back of the courtroom. He bustled genially up to the podium, offering profuse apologies breathlessly to the Court. Of course, not knowing that the Clerk had just telephoned his own office, he said: "I left Wilmington at 8:30 this morning so as to be here right on time. As luck would have it, I had a flat tire just south of Odessa and thus have been unavoidably delayed. So sorry, Your Honors. Now I will begin my argument, if it pleases..."

The Chief Justice interrupted: "Just a moment, counsel, not so fast if you please."

The Chief Justice and other members of the Court then said nothing for what seemed even to me to be a long time. The stony silence was grim and appalling. Then the Chief Justice gravely looked from left to right at his judicial colleagues and asked in a flat tone: "Which tire went flat?" The surprised attorney replied with fear and trembling in his voice: "Why do you ask?" The Chief Justice replied: "This Court is always interested in matters that affect the performance of officers of this Court." The attorney thought and said: "The right." The Chief Justice said: "Front or back?" The attorney blanched and then said, "Front" and then added: "I think."

The Chief Justice and the other two on the bench savored this flat lie in total silence for another awesome length of time. Finally the Chief Justice said with deliberation: "Very well. For the present at least, let us proceed with the argument in this case, lest we delay those attorneys who have managed to avoid having flats south of Odessa." The ominous way in which he pronounced these words struck fear and trembling into my own wicked little heart. I decided right then and there to make a new beginning since it was plain here that at least the full unvarnished truth was all that would pass muster. (Little did I know that very shortly I was going to have occasion to carry out that recently acquired precept and discard some of the more liberal approaches to veracity that had been my style at times in school, at home, and elsewhere).

Actually, in view of the above horrible little curtain-raiser, I have entirely forgotten what the first appeal itself was all about. I do remember that the attorney who had been there on time had tried unsuccessfully to wipe a certain smirk off his face arising from the satisfaction of knowing that he and the Court were sharing a secret. Thus, the unfortunate liar launched into his argument, trying by his sincerity, legal knowledge, and wit to convince the Court of the merit of his client's case. However, I recall learning that the client of the attorney who was late did not get penalized. The Court decided in favor of the client though I later heard it whispered about that the Court administered the liar a blistering reprimand in private.

As the first argument drew to a close, I looked over at my opponent. He did not have on a starched, white shirt: instead, he was wearing a sort of a ratty gray-blue shirt, the collar tips of which curled up. By this time, I had begun to feel just a tad better. The Chief Justice courteously apologized to me and my colleague for the delay: he said that, if it was agreeable to us, the Court would feel more comfortable with a five minute recess. After the Court had filed out, my opponent leered over at me the way a wolf does at a lone sheep when he discovers the shepherd is away. He said craftily, "Well, sonny boy, and just where is your learned parent?" When I disclosed that my father was flat on his back and that I would be making the argument, his grin broadened: he could taste blood. His satisfaction annoyed me so I decided to try to have a little sport of my own with my opponent. Just as the Court was about to come back on the bench again, I slid alongside him as he stood waiting at the podium, ready to begin his argument. I said quietly: "Excuse me, but I think your fly is ever so slightly open." He never even looked down. Instead, he looked venomously at me and hissed back: "Young fella, you can't catch me with the oldest trick in the book. But just for that, I am going to call the Court's attention to the fact that you could not have shepardized two main cases. I might otherwise have overlooked that failing but for this dirty little trick you tried to play on me." Further exchanges were cut short as the three members of the Court again regally trooped back through the door and sat down. Of course, my opponent had put his legal rapier at exactly the place where I was most vulnerable: I had not indeed shepardized our two most important cases. But how did that old wolf know that? The Chief Justice duly asked if counsel was ready for the argument. We both replied "Ready." I must say that what my opponent had just said made me so nervous that I did consider for an instant whether I should blurt out that I was not ready (indeed not at all ready).

Well, my worthy opponent launched into his argument with a half-bow to the Court. He said cringingly: "May it please the Court?" He then recited all of the usual reasons why the Court might hold that this general release was not a general release at all. To my secret pleasure, the members of the Court looked uninterested. However, just before my opponent was about to sit down, his tone and manner turned as unctuous as Uriah Heap. Looking slyly at me in a brief sidelong glance, he said in most deferential tones: "Now I know that my young colleague is a graduate of the great and well-known Harvard Law School and not an old graduate of a humble night law school like myself. Thus, I am sure that he shepardized each and every one of the cases cited in his brief. But for his distinguished legal pedigree, I would have thought that one of the principal cases or perhaps two that he has cited in his brief just might have been overruled. Perhaps they were just questioned in later decisions. But I am sure my brilliant young friend would not offer cases to this, the highest Court of this State, if in fact there were later authorities that overruled or questioned one of his cases." As he went back to sit down, he gave me a wicked half smile.

I am sure that I blushed or went pale. I wished that I had shepardized *all* of the cases carefully as I had been instructed to do! I did not, of course, know if one or two of the unshepardized cases might have been overruled or questioned by later decisions. They both seemed sound enough to me though, of course, I knew nothing about the law of releases.

I didn't have too long to stew or fret over this legal quandary that my opponent had put me in. All too soon, far too soon, it was my turn to stand up and approach the lectern. However, as I was about to get up and go to the lectern, I saw that the insurance manager was already at the podium. I was horrified at first but quickly thought that fate perhaps had intervened to save me from impending disgrace. Perhaps he was inspired by our cause or perhaps fired up by Schenley, or perhaps at long last he saw his one opportunity to show the world his wasted gifts as an appellate advocate. In any case, he began:

"Learned Judges of the highest Court of the State of Delaware, I am going to make the argument since our lawyer, William Prickett, Sr., is flat on his back with a war wound and this youngster does not know a general release from a hold harmless agreement. Why—"

At this point, the Chief Justice interrupted and inquired if this would-be Daniel Webster was a duly authorized member of the Bar of the State of Delaware.

When the insurance manager ruefully admitted that he was not a member of the Bar, the Chief Justice said:

"Well in that case, you do not have the right to be heard. We will hear from the young Mr. Prickett and hear whether he has anything to say that will shed some helpful light and learning on the murky subject at hand—the scope and effect of a general release."

Sadly, my savior relinquished the podium and (equally sadly) I took his place. But, my client whispered: "Go get 'em, tiger!" and slapped me on the back as we traded places. Whatever thought I had on the subject of releases had been quite scattered by all that had thus far gone on. However, there was nothing to do but launch bravely into the argument. In point of fact, my argument at that point consisted principally of reiterating various legal platitudes that I had picked up out of various legal garbage cans. For example, I told the Court: "A litigant who comes to the appellate court armed with a jury verdict is in the strongest position known to the law." The Chief Justice listened to me repeat that nonsense about three times. He then remarked with just a touch of sarcasm: "Yes, Mr. Prickett, we have heard you run through that old nostrum three times by my count, though I may have missed some. We get your point, minor though it is. The phrase, I believe, was originally that of Stephen Decatur. You might have had the courtesy at least of acknowledging the source. I am something of a student of that American hero. Mr. Decatur was known for his patriotism rather than his legal brilliance, particularly on the rather dry subject of the scope of general releases which is all we are considering today. Stephen Decatur also said: 'My country right or wrong'. Incidentally, since we have gotten off on Stephen Decatur, you may also be interested in another of the sayings of Stephen Decatur: 'The law is that which is stoutly asserted and boldly maintained'. It's a pity you didn't throw that into your argument since it seems to be one of the principal basis of your argument."

At one point, referring to a recently decided case, I said: "The Supreme Court has recently held in *Spalding v. Central Railroad- —*". The Chief Justice held up his hand and leaned over the bench. He peered owlishly over his glasses, raised his eyebrows and said with feigned astonishment and incredulity: "My goodness, Mr. Prickett, for the life of me, I do not recall that this Court has ever decided a case by that name. Do any other members of the Court recall such a case?" The Justices duly shook their heads (clearly, they had participated in this sort of judicial snipe hunt before).

"Oh," I said hastily, "I'm referring to the Supreme Court of the United States." The Chief Justice paused and said: "Young man, here in Delaware, when reference is made to 'the Supreme Court', we assume that whoever is using the phrase is referring to this Court and not some other Court that is said to sit in the District of Columbia." Letting that sink in, he added: "The Court in the District of Columbia is a court in a collateral system of justice. What that Court says is at times legally significant and at other times not at all significant, particularly when that Court issues nine different opinions. Nevertheless, we now understand what Court you were trying to refer to and will accord the decision of that Court only the weight that it merits in view of the source."

Then Justice Wolcott said: "Mr. Prickett, your colleague seems to suggest that there just might be one or two of the cases cited in your brief that has been overruled or at least questioned. However, he assures us that he at least relied on you to have shepardized the cases you cite. However, he doesn't say flatly that some of your cases have been overruled or questioned. Would you please assure the Court that each and every one of the cases cited in your brief has in fact been shepardized and that none of the decisions have been overruled or questioned."

Now was when my recent lesson in candor came to my immediate rescue. Overcoming a propensity in my youth to fib, I said as manfully as I could: "Your Honors, to my great embarrassment, I have to admit to this Court that I neglected to carry out my father's direction to shepardize all cases cited in our brief. There were two cases I could not shepardize: some of the pages from Shepard's had been removed from the County Law Library's volumes. Now I know I should have gone to the DuPont Company library, but I did not take the time to do so."

The Chief Justice having heard my pitiful account said with a mock mournful sigh: "Oh dear, that just means that we overworked judges must now do the attorneys' work. Young man, we must now shepardize your cases as you could and should have done." I was close to tears.

However, Justice Tunnell, who had been enjoying the game, now spoke up and said: "Now, now, Chief Justice, I do not think that will be at all necessary. I have in fact already shepardized the cases cited by both parties including the two cases as to which the pages in Shepard's were torn out by someone last week. I can assure the worried young attorney for the appellant who neglected to shepardize those two cases that none of the cases cited in his brief have been questioned or overruled. On the other hand, I did find that there are two cases cited by the attorney for the appellee, one of which is miscited and one of which was overruled some ten years ago." Quite suddenly, the sun came out. The tables had been turned and the hunter was now the hunted.

Well, this little horror story eventually came to an end. The Court had not strictly adhered to its rule on time. I guess that the three of the Justices had tacitly decided amongst themselves that they were not going to get much help from the two attorneys appearing in front of them. They proceeded to throw the legal ball about general releases back and forth among themselves occasionally asking me or my colleague whether we agreed on a particular point. Thus, they had a lively discussion among themselves, almost totally ignoring us, there being no one else in the courtroom other than the Clerk and my client.

The Chief Justice then courteously thanked both of us for the argument saying that it had been a help to the Court in several different ways. He concluded the Court would in due course render its decision.

When I came back to Wilmington, I drove immediately to my father's house. To my great pleasure, I found that the acute episode was over. The nerve spasm had passed. In a day or so my father would be back in legal harness again. My father questioned me closely with professional interest about the argument. I told him the whole unvarnished truth. He was amused at all that had happened to me. When I told him about why I had not shepardized the two important cases (because the pages were missing) he said, "I always suspected that fellow cut pages out of library books but your experience confirms it."

Suddenly I realized what my opponent had done. I said, "That's how he knew I had been unable to shepardize them."

My father replied, "Of course. Justice Tunnell realized that as well."

In due course, the Supreme Court handed down its landmark opinion in *Hockem v. Rising Sun Trucking Co.* My father read it with great professional interest (and paternal pride) since the Court had adopted all of our views on the scope and effect of general releases. Of course, I knew very well that I had precious little to do with the result or with the opinion. Aside from those who read this little account, the world will never know that the genesis of the law on general releases here in Delaware at least does not stem from my scholarly efforts or my oral advocacy. I am quite content to leave it just that way.

I did learn a great deal from this initial argument, including the importance of white shirts, shepardizing cases, becoming familiar with all of the briefs, practicing an oral argument, getting a good night's sleep the night before and not drinking rye whiskey on the way down to an argument. I also learned that candor pays off and that the function of an attorney in an oral argument is to try really to provide the Justices hearing the argument with some further insight into the issues and questions which they have to decide correctly. Perhaps what I learned so painfully may be of service to younger colleagues.

# Scull & Heap

From the title of this small effort, some readers might be licking their literary chops thinking that they have stumbled, however implausibly, on a pirate story along the lines of Howard Pyle's *Book of Pirates* that delighted us so much in the far off days of our youth. Perhaps some readers may think from the title that this is a medical treatise or horror story. On the other hand, a literary reader might think that this is some sort of a scholarly dissertation on the Dickens character "Uriah Heap." Wrong, wrong—all dead wrong. None of the above is even vaguely close. Furthermore, if the reader backtracks and notes the spelling of the title, the careful reader probably can figure out this slow starting tale refers to none of the above.

Rather, this is an account based on my recollections about a giant black and white print that Nicholas Scull, who was the King's Surveyor General for the Commonwealth of Pennsylvania in 1753, and his colleague, George Heap, who was an engraver, drew, published, and sold. In a word, they drew a dramatic view of the City of Philadelphia from the Jersey shore in 1753. This is a story about one of eight or nine copies that are still in existence. Now, hold on: do not throw this little essay in the trash can or into the gutter and turn the T.V. on to watch "Wheel of Fortune" and Vanna White's captivating legs. This account has some tidbits that are guaranteed to tickle the fancy of at least readers with some cultural pretensions. For example, it includes how a well known New York art gallery was outsmarted or outnegotiated by a country lawyer from Delaware (my father). It also includes an account of how a high official of the Internal Revenue Service lost his nerve, playing "chicken," with another Delaware lawyer (guess who!). And, it has a smashing conclusion: one copy of the print in question ended up where it certainly belongs.

But, let's start with a few background facts. First, as all reasonably educated Americans know, in 1753, Philadelphia was the second largest city in the British Empire. It was absolutely owned and controlled by Thomas and Richard Penn, the proprietors of Pennsylvania. In order to market Philadelphia and the Pennsylvania Commonwealth, the Penns retained Messrs. Scull and Heap to make a large print of their handsome city. Thus, Scull and Heap rowed themselves over to the Jersey shore across from "Philly" (as those from Camden were apt even then to call the City of Brotherly Love). The print shows basically all of what has now been so beautifully restored in the Society Hill section of Philadlephia today. In the foreground, sailing on the Delaware River, are a plethora of little boats as well as sea-going ships. The print itself shows the skyline of Philadelphia as it existed in Ben Franklin's youth: its church steeples, houses, warehouses, docks, and other commercial establishments. Implausibly, there is a rather large windmill built right out in the river. Below the print there is a written inscription describing (and "plugging") the land, industry, and trade of the City of Philadelphia.

The Scull and Heap print is about seven feet long and two feet high. Apparently, it was widely distributed in England, Scotland, and Ireland to attract and recruit colonists to the New World. However, because of its immense size, most copies of the Scull and Heap print were chopped up or used to wrap fish. Very few of these "elephant-size" prints survived to the present. At the time our account really gets underway, copies were scarce indeed—there were only seven or eight left in the whole wide world. Thus, they were and are a real rarity— that is, provided you were interested in such graphic monsters.

Of course, I, as a feckless young lawyer, knew absolutely nothing at all of the Pennsylvania history that I now so urbanely recount. Certainly, I had never heard of Scull or Heap or knew that the City of Brotherly Love was the second biggest city in the British Empire. Indeed, having graduated from Princeton and Harvard Law School, I doubt that I knew that the Commonwealth of Pennsylvania was part of the British Empire at the time: ignorance was youthful bliss.

However, one fine day in New York my father and I were walking back from a deposition. I had watched my father tear a hapless witness apart. Suddenly my father stopped in front of the window of a large, well known art gallery on Fifth Avenue. He grabbed my arm. I thought that something dramatic had happened, like a robbery or a lady taking off all of her clothes. (Something like that would have been of some interest to me at that time, and indeed still might.) Nothing of the kind: instead, my father pointed to a large black and white "picture" displayed on an easel in the window. He said to me,

"My God, that's the Scull & Heap print!" I replied, sort of lackadaisi-
cally, "Oh, really?", thinking quite seriously about just how good a
steely cold martini would taste if I could just get my father on back to
the Princeton Club.

But my father took me even more firmly by the arm and quick-
stepped me on into the gallery. A dignified young man in a morning
coat and pinstripe trousers minced up to us. He lazily inquired in a
snotty tone of voice as to whether he could be of service, clearly
implying by his manner and his tone that he could not possibly
conceive how two such country bumpkins could have any possible
interest in anything in his high-tone gallery. My father was not put off
at all by the young man's airs. Instead, he came right to the point,
saying, "Young man, I see you have a copy of the Scull & Heap print in
the window."

"Yes", the young clerk replied somewhat haughtily. "It's a beautiful
copy. It's one of the few left." My father inquired the price. The clerk
was somewhat surprised at this direct approach and replied that it was
"X" thousand dollars. My father shook his head and said, "Young
man, I am prepared to offer this gallery one-half of the price in cash
here today." The young man looked as shocked as if a dish of cold
water had been thrown in his smug little puss and replied somewhat
indignantly, "Our gallery doesn't deal that way."

My father replied, "Nonsense, young man! Get me your manager."
The little snit wiggled away. Presently the aristocratic-looking
manager came on the scene: he spoke with a distinctly English accent,
though I now suspect he probably was born and raised in Kansas or
some place thereabout. My father repeated his offer to this somewhat
more urbane art dealer. Clearly, he was interested in making a sale but
he told my father that the print was for sale but only at the stated price.
He said that the fact that my father recognized the print meant that
my father clearly understood that it was only one of nine or ten Scull &
Heap prints left in the world, that it was a great bargain at that price,
and that surely a "real collector" would come in and snap it up. My
father replied, "Ah, well, but it's been in your window for some time,
hasn't it? No one has snapped it up yet, have they?" The floor manager
made his first mistake—he paused ever so slightly but then grudgingly
admitted that that was true. My father turned to go and said, "Well, is
my offer refused?" The dealer made a second mistake—he hesitated
again but then reluctantly affirmed that the asking price was firm.

With that, my father turned on his heel and, motioning me, walked
firmly on out. I was mortified. I told my father when I got him safely
out on the street that I was ashamed to be with him. I pointed out that

he had haggled like a veritable Armenian rug merchant in a bazaar. My father told me firmly that I was a young idiot. He said that anybody who knows what he's doing, especially in the art world, always negotiates. "If you do not do so, the person on the other side would take you for a fool or an American or both. For goodness sake, can't you think of anything beyond your next martini?" (Just how did he know that was what I had been thinking about!) "Why not pay attention. Perhaps you just might learn a little bit about history and the art of successful negotiation!"

My father then said that he would bet me a week of my pay that he would end up with the print. I had long since learned never, never to bet with my father. Besides, I certainly needed every cent and more of the princely sum of $45.00 a week that my father paid me for six and a half days of law work that I did for him.

Well, the following week, my father was back in New York. He told me on his return that he had gone by the gallery and saw that the Scull & Heap print was no longer in the window. However, he had gone in and had spoken directly to the manager. My father said he had begun by remarking that the print was no longer in the window. He then got the dealer to make a third mistake: he admitted that the print had not been sold but had been put back into inventory. My father then said that, while he had been willing to offer half of the stated price the week before, he was now cutting his price by an additional $250.00. The manager looked pained: again, the floor manager hesitated but reluctantly declined my father's lowered offer.

Several weeks later, my father and I were in New York. We were there for depositions but I knew my father well enough to know that he was hot on the trail of the Scull & Heap print and that was one of the real purposes of our trip to New York. After I had cross-examined an evasive witness under the careful guidance of my father, we trotted briskly on over to the gallery. My father told me on the way that he would be able to tell immediately whether he was going to get the print by the manner in which we were greeted. This time, when we came on into the gallery, we were greeted amiably by the original clerk. He now came forward, exclaiming with an ingratiating smile, "Oh, Messrs. Prickett, Pere et fils, how nice to see you again." We were welcomed equally effusively by the aristocratic manager. My father promptly got down to business as any astute Armenian rug merchant would. Thus, my father said, "I am tempted at this point to cut another $250.00 from my offer of several weeks ago." The manager could not conceal a wince. "However, I will not do so", my father said with a definite air of magnaminity. "I will in fact renew my offer for a last time but only provided it is accepted forthwith, with no further quibbling. Understood?" The floor manager protested that the print was worth a good deal more, etc., etc., but in the end he said that the offer was accepted. He went on to justify the gallery's acceptance by saying the gallery was interested in having the Scull & Heap print in the possession of someone who clearly knew the artistic merit and historical significance of the print. However, my father was not interested in "bells and whistles": he now owned the print. However, he wanted every last jot and tittle of his pound of artistic flesh: he insisted that the rather handsome black and gilt frame be thrown in by the gallery, pointing out that the gallery would have no possible use for the frame since they had now sold him the print. He also got them to agree to ship the print down to Delaware at their cost, including the insurance. The manager rather ruefully remarked as we said good-bye (and got an "au revoir" and a little wave from the clerk) that my father was a hard bargainer. Of course, I could have told him that from the outset. (Indeed, quite a number of other people learned that fact both before and after that particular afternoon.)

Be that as it may, my father was quietly ecstatic, not only at having acquired the print but at having outnegotiated a large prestigious New York gallery. (He did spring later for a martini or two.) Of course, killjoy that I was, I tried to temper his keen pleasure by pointing out to him that he had taken quite a risk: after all, somebody else could have come along and bought the print right out from under his fine Armenian nose. Then, where would he have been? First, my father calmly pointed out that he was used to taking risks. Second, he said that if he had not gotten the print, he would have been no worse off for having tried. Finally, he put me firmly in my place, saying that the print was a bargain, even at the original price: from the outset he was determined to have the print and would have paid the full original price or even a tad more—"So, there, Mr. Smarty Pants!" (Of course, that was the reason he was so ready to make a bet that he would end up with the print.) He then presented the print to me as a paternal gift, gruffly justifying the gift by saying he saw no reason why the print should swell his estate.

Some weeks afterwards, the gallery manager anxiously called up. Was there any chance that my father would part with the print, of course at a profit? The inquiry stemmed from the fact that Independence Hall in Philadelphia, run by the National Park Service, now desperately wanted that very print. The Park Service somehow found it had the funds to buy the print. I was all for a sale at a profit (i.e., my profit since I was the owner of the print). One look from my father was enough to convince me that it had been a very bad idea even to make such a helpful suggestion along these lines. (Who now had the keen nose for a fast artistic buck?, I thought, albeit to myself.) However, it was my father's turn to pause. He told me that the print was really a national treasure and Independence Hall really should have one, perhaps "our" copy. But in the end, my father called the manager and declined..."at least for the present." He said to me, "Someday you really should give that print to Independence Hall." All in all, I learned a good deal from this little episode.

Thereafter, the print was hung in the main conference room of our Wilmington law office. My father never failed when he came into the conference room to shoot a fond sideways glance at his giant print. I also came to think of it as rather handsome. However, it was "pearls before swine" generally. The witnesses who came to face the tortures of depositions could not have cared less. Nor were most of the attorneys in our office wildly concerned about the beauty or historical niceties of the Scull & Heap print of Philadelphia in 1753.

Eventually my father died. Of course, father had made me insure "my" print at double the original price that the gallery had demanded. (Fear Greeks bearing gifts.) The insurance premium kept going up year by year since at least the insurance company understood the value of the Scull & Heap print. Indeed, the premium soaked up a good deal of my pay. I never disclosed the mounting value of the print simply because I was afraid some burglar would get wind of the value of this artistic gem hanging in our office and, instead of taking the typewriters, he might make off with the Scull & Heap print. (That scenario now seems highly implausible as I think back on the burglars who plied their trade in Wilmington, Delaware, in the 1950s.) However, I did have sort of a twinge of conscience about the print. While it looked very handsome in our conference room and I had begun to enjoy it, I knew that this national treasure deserved a better place to be displayed than in the main conference room of our offices (even though our offices were located in the Starr House dating from 1802). Indeed, a couple of collectors heard about the print and attempted to "steal" it from me (a little bit along the lines of the way Manhattan was bought from the Indians). However, since I knew that the print was increasingly valuable, I firmly declined to sell to any private collector.

As I have noted above, I had something of a nagging conscience that told me the print really belonged in Independence Hall. I consulted with a number of print collectors, dealers, and historians: they agreed to a man that I really should donate the print to Independence Hall. Thus, I firmly made up my mind at that point to give the print to Independence Hall. I went on to round up three appraisals that would do something quite handsome for my tax returns by way of deductions for the foreseeable future. Thus, I was urged on by my father's wishes, my own conscience, and with a tax incentive that longed to be satisfied. Any lingering doubts that I might have had vanished when I was assured that, since the Scull & Heap print was a black and white engraving, I could have a photo copy made that would appear to be the genuine thing except to a really discerning artistic eye (of which I can assure you there were damned few that ever came into our offices). In short, I took the original out of the frame and had two copies made by a commercial copyng firm. I gave one to Primitive Hall out in the Unionville hunting country since it seemed not entirely unlikely that there might have been one hanging there before it was cut up and used for scratch paper or something like that. I, of course, retained the other.

Then I somewhat diffidently approached the curators of Independence Hall. Would they be interested, not in buying a copy of the Scull & Heap print but having one donated entirely gratis? Words can hardly describe their amazement, surprise, joy and gratitude. Quite out of the blue (i.e., Delaware), they finally would get a copy of the prized Scull & Heap print for Independence Hall. Wow!

I told the curators I would donate the print provided the IRS would agree to the appraised value of the print (and, hence, my deduction), though I had already decided to give, deduction or no.

In due course, the IRS, which would have to "pay the piper" in terms of the tax deduction for me, duly delegated a fairly high tax official to see the print and pass on its value. He called and made an appointment to come down to see me, see the print, and discuss the proposed deduction. On the appropriate day, this grim tax reaper came in, introduced himself, and glanced casually at the seven-foot document lying on the conference room table and the three written appraisals. I could see at once that he was not nearly as impressed with the print as I was, nor did he agree at all with the appraisals that I had obtained as to the print's value. Of course, this was long before the IRS had its own appraisal service. After some sparring about, he said that he could not really believe that "an old picture of Philly" was worth nearly what was reflected in the appraisals. In fact, he said flatly that he was going to disallow the proposed deduction entirely or cut it way down. I looked him square in the eye and told him plainly that that was his privilege, but if one arm of the United States government was going to quibble on the value of a gift to another arm of the U.S., that it then had the effect of entirely drying up my desire to be generous.

He said sternly, "What do you mean?" I replied: "I have a copy of the print. If the U.S. government really believes the Scull & Heap print is worth nothing, I am going to burn the original. Let me point out to you, sir, that I will make it known that this loss of a national treasure will have occurred because the IRS is too chintzy to appreciate the value of what was to be given to the shrine of our country, Independence Hall." He looked unimpressed by my patriotic oratory. I went on to warn him that if this in fact did happen, it could lead to some unpleasant professional repercussions so far as he personally was concerned. However, I went on, it might be a service to the IRS since, in the future, the IRS would be led to deal on a more reasonable basis with those who wanted to do something handsome for the United States of America. The agent continued to feign total indifference but I detected a fatal moment of hesitation. However, he said, "Well, you do just as you damned well please, but I know what I am going to do. I am going to allow you almost nothing by way of a deduction for that big piece of paper showing nothing more than the skyline of Philly a couple of hundred years ago. So there!"

All this occurred at a time before I quit smoking. I therefore pulled out my trusty Bic lighter and flicked it open. I went over to the print, which, as I say, was lying on the table. I said quietly to the agent, "I am going to count to ten. If you don't have the good sense to rethink your position or rather the position of the government, at the end of that count, you and I will have the sultry pleasure of watching and smelling this national treasure go up in smoke and flames right here and now before your very own eyes. Understand?" He hesitated but said with false bravado, "You don't mean it."

My reply was, "Oh, yeah? Well just you wait and see." I then began to count. "One, two, three ..." At the count of six, I could see in his eyes that he was thinking of "caving" but he still wasn't ready to throw his hand in quite yet. At the count of ten, I lit one tiny corner of the print: the "national treasure" was alight and burning. He walked quickly over and blew out the flame. One corner was slightly charred. He said, "You win, son. But, by the Living God, your tax returns better be dead right for the next twenty-five years." He then stalked on out.

Of course, I had only "torched" a copy. As my father had remarked, life is full of risks and one of the pleasures is in successfully running a risk.

Well, the original of the Scull & Heap print, of course, is hanging on the landing of the steps to the second floor of Independence Hall. On the other hand, in our main conference room, there is a framed photocopy of the Scull & Heap print: one corner has a small imperceptible burn mark on it. I come into the conference room from time to time. Each time, I glance over at my copy of the Scull & Heap print with a sort of double satisfaction. Nobody else cares very much.

# Why I Sometimes Wear
## Red Suspenders on Tuesdays

**I** am quite often asked why I sometimes wear firemen's suspenders on Tuesdays. Usually, I give a deadpan reply, "Why, to hold up my pants!" That answer, while correct, and a somewhat smarty-pants answer, is really not the whole truth. If the reader for some inexplicable reason would like to know the whole truth about why I sometimes wear red suspenders on Tuesdays, then it is necessary to wade through this whole effort unless the reader is an intellectual chiseler by nature or training; a cheater will flip right to the end and learn this reason why I usually wear, etc. But, as the great Chinese literary critic, Lin Sung, so wisely remarked at the end of the Hung Period, "In any decent sandwich, the meat is always between the slices of bread." Thus, the reader who wants the real meatball, if there is one, has got to read this whole damn piece, okay? (But, there is also a thin slice of Thucydides, as a sort of classic pickle to spice up this homely American literary sandwich.)

Recently, the entire Bench and Bar of Delaware, Princeton University, the American Judicature Society, and a number of other organizations have striven to outdo one another in heaping honors on the head of an outstanding Delaware lawyer, E. N. Carpenter, II. I have been among those who have enjoyed seeing Ned reap in his lifetime the deserved praise for all of his many accomplishments. Indeed, Delaware and all of its people owe Ned a huge debt, which they will never really know about or be able to repay: Ned, forsaking national office and wider fields of endeavor in which he would undoubtedly have excelled, preferred to stay on in his native Delaware. He worked as a lawyer and, in a very real sense, as a servant of this very small state and all of its people. Thus, as he reached three score and ten, it was entirely appropriate that his home state and those who have enjoyed the benefits of his hard work and intelligence over all these years should pause and pay him deserved homage.

When the incense clears, it should be remembered that Ned was and is after all a Delaware trial lawyer. This, then, is a little account to recall that Ned, like every other lawyer, did occasionally have (if only very occasionally) a professional reverse or two along the way: indeed, every serious trial lawyer does lose a close case now and then. But it will be seen that the plaintiffs' defeat in this particular case was not Ned's fault: it was due mostly to Ned's out-of-state colleague and a most unpleasant client. Still, Ned made one mistake and it was a fatal one: he was just too gracious. Let me quickly add that the plaintiffs' defeat was not in any way as a result of my puny efforts: I was really a bystander. Actually, Everett F. Warrington, Esquire of Georgetown, was the wily architect of the plaintiffs' and Ned's defeat.

Of course, this account is only my recollection of what happened. Others, including Ned himself, may recall things quite differently. Probably, the true facts (whatever that means) are irretrievably lost in the mists of time. On the other hand, the facts may have been quite different from the impressions of each of us at the time. So be it: here, then, for what they are worth, are my recollections.

The attorney who bested the plaintiffs, as I said, is a deceased Delaware lawyer by the name of Everett F. Warrington, Esquire. Mr. Warrington was born in Hollyville, a small town near Georgetown in Sussex County, Delaware. For a crossroads in the piney woods of lower Delaware, Georgetown and its environs have been an amazingly fertile source of legal giants. Indeed, a list of great Delaware lawyers and Judges who originally came from Georgetown could take up this whole tale. (Ned himself has Sussex County roots.) But, this tale is, after all, not about Sussex County lawyers generally but about one very crafty old Sussex County trial lawyer, Mr. Warrington, and Ned and his snooty but incompetent out-of-state colleague.

My father told me that Mr. Warrington had not returned to his native Sussex County after law school: rather, he had sought and found legal success in the big city—New York. There Mr. Warrington had a very successful career as an insurance company attorney. However, Mr. Warrington had a taste for rye whiskey, like some other attorneys from Sussex County (and indeed, unfortunately, all too many Delaware attorneys both before and since Mr. Warrington). Thus, Mr. Warrington's New York legal career had been suddenly truncated. A legal Icarus, he had toppled from New York's lofty legal heights. Mr. Warrington had spiraled back down to earth and landed, plunk, in his native Sussex County. When he had recovered somewhat,

Mr. Warrington got himself admitted to the Delaware Bar and turned to a country trial practice. Thus, Everett F. Warrington, Esquire, late in life, with the rasping voice of a man who has wrestled many a night with alcohol, came to be a fixture in the trial courts of Sussex County. Mr. Warrington did not care much what sort of a case it was, criminal or civil—they were all grist for Everett's fierce advocacy.

Mr. Warrington's particular domain was the Superior Court of Sussex County. My father, a Wilmington trial lawyer, at times traveled down to Sussex County to try civil cases there against various Sussex County lawyers, including Mr. Warrington. Mr. Warrington was an astute and able practitioner. My father was an aggressive trial lawyer, but his trademark was careful and thorough preparation of both the law and the facts in every case he tried. Mr. Warrington's swash-buckling style was entirely different. All Mr. Warrington really needed was a client whose cause Mr. Warrington believed in. Without very much preparation at all on either the law or the facts, Mr. Warrington would do his very best to convince a jury to find for his client.

After Harvard Law School, I became the junior attorney in my father's office. Early one Tuesday morning in January, shortly after I was admitted (a year late as some readers may remember), the telephone rang. I was in my father's office at the time. The booming raspy voice on the telephone could be none other than that of Everett F. Warrington. The conversation went something like this:

"Bill, can you hear me? This is Everett Warrington. I am up here in Wilmington to defend a case against a lawyer from Hartford, Connecticut, name of O. B. Priscott. Because of his style, I call him 'prissy,' but not to his face, mind you. He really does not know his elbow from second base. Prissy thinks that he has a hell of a plaintiff's case. I'm defending for the insurance company. There is also a young Delaware lawyer in the case. I have a feeling he at least is very energetic and able. I am not worried a bit about Mr. Prissy, but Mr. Carpenter is a different sort of cat, don't you think?

"Yes, you say you know Ned? You say he is a capable young lawyer who went to Harvard Law School. Prissy also went there.

"Well, be that as it may, but Prissy has not got much of a case so far as I can see. It involves traumatic neurosis, whatever the hell that is. Yes, I'm up here in Wilmington to try the case starting this morning. I wonder if you would have the time to come up to Court today and sort of lend me a hand. Prissy has kind of worn me down with damned fool interrogatories, production, and all that sort of thing. But I am up here now for trial—fact is, as I said, trial starts later this morning. Like you when you come down to Sussex County, I am sort of a country fish out of the water up here in Wilmington."

My father looked aghast. He had a mountain of work to do. He could not suddenly drop everything and stroll over to court for three days as some Sussex County lawyers were apt to do in those halcyon days. My father replied gravely:

"Everett, I am honored to be asked, especially by someone who finished four years of law at St. James College. But I happen to be very busy for the next couple of days: things I simply cannot put off. However, my young son, Bill, was just admitted. He also went to Harvard Law School. Now, Everett, don't hold that against him. Of course, he doesn't have any trial experience at all but maybe he can help you with the papers. I will tell him not to get in your way.

Everett replied: "Oh, well, Bill, send your young man on up. He can't hurt anything. He and I will see what we can do for Mr. Carpenter and Prissy and their traumatic and neurotic lady plaintiff. Thanks, Bill, I appreciate the loan of your son."

My father hung up the phone. He turned to me and told me to get into a white shirt and go up and do what I could to help Mr. Warrington. He said to me:

"Now, Mr. Warrington may have seen brighter days but, mark my words, young man, there is no better lawyer before a jury in the whole State of Delaware. Though he is dramatic and flamboyant, you can learn some things from Mr. Warrington if you can manage to get over your snootiness at having gone to Harvard Law School. In fact, you might just find out something about how to try a jury case."

I could tell my father basically disapproved of Mr. Warrington and his bravado style. Therefore, almost instinctively, I was fully prepared to like Mr. Warrington's way of trying a case.

My father continued, "But, pay close attention to Ned. His style is the direct opposite of that of Mr. Warrington—diligent, thorough, and fully prepared. You'll learn a lot from him if you just take the trouble to do so. I have, of course, never heard of Mr. Priscott.

My father added, "Mr. Warrington still drinks more than he should. Furthermore, like you, Mr. Warrington has the filthy habit of smoking cigarettes."

My father exclaimed indignantly, "Mr. Warrington even smokes in the Courtroom, though it is strictly forbidden to do so. He stamps his digusting cigarette butts out right on the floor underneath the counsel table. It's a disgrace! Don't ever let me or one of the Judges catch you doing that, do you hear, young man?"

"Yes, Father," I replied. (In those days, we did what we were told. Besides, I was trying for the 19th time to quit.) My father concluded, "Now, go on up to Mansure & Prettyman and get yourself a pair of white shirts: you may charge them to my account." I went and bought two new white shirts and hurried up to the Courthouse and into Courtroom No. 1. There was red-faced Mr. Warrington, leaning back in a chair at the defense table, inhaling deeply on a Lucky Strike cigarette. He had a mane of disheveled white hair, a big chest, a short bull neck, and broad shoulders. The tabs of the collar of his somewhat faded blue shirt were curled up. His dark blue suit was a trifle shiny and there were some cigarette ashes scattered down the front of his suit. His pants were held up by both an old leather belt and faded red fireman's suspenders. His tie had a large spot on it. He wore black boots that laced up above his ankles. Mr. Warrington said in a loud rasping voice:

"Well, Sonny Boy, I'm mighty glad to see you. We really do not have much of a defense in this case when all is said and done. Maybe young Mr. Prissy and his colleague, Mr. Carpenter, will overtry their case. Let's hope so anyway. I hope Prissy handles most of their case rather than Ned: I do not think a Delaware jury will cotton to that stuck-up Yankee." I said to Mr. Warrington:

"Sir, may I please look at the pleading file to get some idea of what this case is all about?"

Mr. Warrington laughed and replied with a twinkle:

"Of course, Sonny Boy, here it all is."

He picked up his battered old leather briefcase. He turned it upside down on the counsel table. Out spilled a mass of crumpled papers— complaint, answer, motions, statements, photographs—a messy pile of papers about a foot high. Mr. Warrington smiled at my surprised look and said:

"My secretary, Miss Betts, was supposed to have straightened this mess out. She somehow never quite gets around to such jobs. But, the complaint and answer are someplace in there. So is everything else. Go to it, if you like."

Mr. Warrington then said:

"Sonny Boy, your father tells me you went to Harvard Law School and that this is your first jury trial. That's fine. I'll tell you what we'll do: we will handle this trial together. I will tell you as we go along which of the plaintiffs' witnesses I will cross and which you will cross-examine. Okay with you?"

I was dumbfounded, but delighted. I quickly tried to sort the papers into piles so that I could at least scan the important ones. It was quite impossible to get them in any sort of order: there just was not enough time. Implausibly, at least to my way of thinking, at the very bottom of the pike, there was a battered and soiled copy of Thucydides, "History of the Peloponnesian Wars," in Greek. Just at that moment, Ned Carpenter strode athletically into the courtroom followed by a fastidious young lawyer, already prematurely balding, who sort of trotted along at Ned's heels. Mr. Carpenter's colleague's eye lit on the battered copy of Thucydides in Greek lying before me on the counsel table. He smiled and said, "Look, Ned, are they reading Thucydides in preparation for this trial?"

I replied, "Not me. I've never heard of the gentleman before today." I then added, with the leer of the true ignoramus, "It's all Greek to me. It's Mr. Warrington's book."

Ned said, "Well, I myself need the translation: I never did find the time to learn Greek as I should have. But I guess that failure will not have any effect on the proceedings that bring us together, will it?"

Mr. Warrington's response to this exchange was to say privately to me, "Thucydides contains many examples of the folly of hubris." I nodded in agreement, privately deciding to look up "hubris" later.

Behind Mr. Carpenter and Prissy sailed the large lady plaintiff prominently displaying a gleaming white neck brace. Behind her, her husband slinked in, a timid little rabbit of a man. The plaintiff's team sat down at their table. Ned unloaded six massive black trial notebooks and his spiral notebook from three tidy leather trial briefcases. The notebooks, for which Ned was already well known, were clearly labeled and indexed. Ned opened Notebook Number One. I was standing beside him: there was "The Plaintiff's Opening," all typed out, underlined, and with exclamation marks. Prepared: wow!

I asked Mr. Warrington behind my hand, " Where is our truck driver defendant?" Mr. Warrington replied quietly:

"Well, Sonny Boy, between us, the fact is I never could quite catch up with that rascal. He is known all over Sussex County as Crazy Jim, probably because he is cross-eyed and somewhat wild. His common-law wife, Lydia Mae, and the Sheriff of Sussex County have all been chasing all around trying to find Crazy Jim. None of us ever found out where he was until a day or so ago. Then, a State Trooper happened to shoot Crazy Jim in the gut as he was trying to break into a gas station late Sunday night. Jim still has a .38 calibre bullet in his stomach. That bullet and a criminal charge are keeping him in the Beebe Hospital just for the moment. Jim is not going to be able to show up for this trial, thank goodness. We'll just have to get along without him. Not to worry, okay?"

Just then, the Chief Bailiff intoned in a solemn official voice: "All rise. All those having business before this Court draw nigh and they shall be heard. God save the State of Delaware and this Honorable Court. Court is now in session." The small door behind the Bench opened and the Judge walked in. The panel of jurors was ushered in under the watchful eyes of the Chief Bailiff and his tipstaffs. The Court had the Prothonotary announce the case.

Mr. Carpenter said, "If it please the Court, may I present and move the admission of O. B. Priscott, Esquire, Connecticut. Mr. Priscott was a classmate of mine at Harvard Law School. Mr. Priscott and I, with the Court's permission will present the plaintiff's case jointly."

The Court was about to graciously welcome Mr. Priscott and grant Mr. Carpenter's motion when Mr. Warrington stood up and said, "Your Honor, may I be heard?"

The Judge looked surprised and clearly annoyed. Motions for admission pro hac vice were granted as a matter of course at that time. Thus, the Court said, "No, Mr. Warrington, you may not be heard."

Mr. Warrington said, "Well, now, Your Honor, hold on, if Your Honor please. Down where I come from in Sussex County, an attorney is entitled to be heard as a matter of right on any motion. But, Your Honor, I was not going to challenge Mr. Carpenter's motion as to Mr. Priss, or Mr. Priscott, or whatever his name is, though Mr. Carpenter did not state that his colleague was in good standing in Connecticut or wherever he comes from."

Mr. Priscott got angrily to his feet and blurted out, "Your Honor, I resent that: of course, I am in good standing in Connecticut!" Mr. Warrington: "Hold on, sir. Don't go getting your New England dander up. I never said you weren't in good standing. For all I know, you are. I just said Mr. Carpenter had not assured the Judge you were. But, what I got up to do was to make my own motion. When I heard that there were not one but two lawyers from the Harvard Law School against my poor client, Jim, I decided I better get myself a Harvard Law School lawyer. Young Mr. Prickett here beside me has finally gotten admitted to the Bar. I have associated him with me for the trial of this case. Mr. Prickett also went to Harvard Law School. However, Your Honor, as you can see, it was still two Harvard Law School lawyers against one. I just wondered if Mr. Priscott was in good standing. If by any chance he wasn't, then it would be all even so far as Harvard Law School grads are concerned. But, Your Honor, my colleague and I are quite willing to take both of the plaintiff's Harvard Law School grads on."

The Court relaxed, smiled, and said, "Come, come gentlemen, let's not start off on a dicordant note over how many Harvard Law School graduates each side has. Mr. Priscott and Mr. Prickett, you are both welcome."

The Judge then asked, "Ready for the plaintiff?" Prissy rose and replied in a squeaky voice, "Ready for the plaintiff, Your Honor." The Court turned and said, "Well, and what about you, Mr. Warrington— is the defendant ready?" Mr. Warrington stood up slowly, leaned on his cane and boomed out with just a hint of sarcasm, "Your Honor, the defendant has always been ready to try this particular case. We are still ready. Let's begin."

That was in the good old days when a Delaware jury could be impaneled in ten minutes. But, this time it took a full twenty-five minutes because Prissy, armed with a detailed jury card on each juror, scanned each card and each juryman again and again as they took their place in the box. Prissy exercised each of his six peremptory challenges, as he had every right to do. Each time it was his turn to challenge, Mr. Warrington slowly got up and with thinly disguised disdain and, looking directly at Mr. Priscott, said: "The defendant is still quite, quite satisfied, Your Honor, with the jury as it is now constituted." There were a couple of jurors that I certainly would have stricken, though I knew nothing about jurymen, or trial tactics, or indeed anything at all for that matter. But Mr. Warrington was making it abundantly clear to everyone in the Courtroom that he was not at all finicky which jurors heard and decided the case. The implication was plain: Mr. Warrington was going to win the case no matter which jurors sat.

By this time, I had managed to read the plaintiffs' tidy and detailed complaint and indeed Mr. Warrington's somewhat badly typed answer. It was a fairly straightforward case. Basically, the plaintiff's husband had been driving to the Hotel DuPont in downtown Wilmington when our non-appearing defendant had driven his employer's 18-wheel chicken truck right smack dab into the back of the plaintiff's car. The plaintiffs claimed that their Buick had been stopped for a red light. The truck had pushed the Buick all the way across the intersection and into a fireplug standing on the far side of the intersection. (Our answer asserted that the plaintiff had stopped suddenly on a yellow light rather than going on through.) Neither the plaintiff nor her husband had suffered any broken bones or indeed any cuts or bruises. In fact, the husband was not hurt at all. But the lady alleged she had suffered a simply awful neck injury and traumatic neurosis. Indeed, there was an impressive list of doctors' visits for traumatic neurosis, but $131.00 was the total amount claimed for her medical bills other than for traumatic neurosis. Her husband politely and diffidently alleged loss of his right to his wife's consortium—a polite way that the law (before the Thomas and Kennedy T.V. dramas) used to refer to the fact that the plaintiff's neck was so painful that she was no earthly use to her husband in her matrimonial obligations. However, looking at the lady plaintiff, a scowling middle-aged harridan if I ever saw one, I smiled inwardly, thinking that her little timid husband had not really missed much, if anything, along these lines. In an aside to me, Mr. Warrington had labeled the husband as "Mr. Mousey."

I could have saved myself the trouble of reading the complaint. Prissy turned and bowed deeply to the Judge, and requested with elaborate politeness the required leave of Court to address the jury directly. Then he turned to the jury and explained in exquisite detail just what had happened and how seriously and permanently hurt the plaintiff was as a result of the negligence of our truck driver.

At the end of his explanation, it was obvious to me (and I supposed everyone else) that this was a case of clear liability. The only real question that the jury would have was the amount of the damages: after all, our defendant truck driver had come up to a car stopping for a yellow light which was about to turn red. Our driver had run right into the back of the car in which the plaintiff was riding. What could be clearer?

The Court asked Mr. Warrington if he wanted to make an opening. Mr. Warrington again got slowly to his feet and said to the Court:

"No, thank you, Your Honor. I don't think that's at all necessary at this point. But I would hope someone at some point is going to tell an old country fellow like me just what this so-called traumatic neurosis is really all about. When folks in Sussex County where I come from sue, it's usually over real injuries, such as broken bones."

Mr. Warrington's remark was clearly improper. Prissy half rose to his feet to object. Prissy looked at Ned who shook his head imperceptibly. Prissy caught the signal and sank back into his seat.

Prissy first called our defendant truck driver as an adverse witness, again as he had every right to do.

Mr. Warrington said evenly,

"Sorry, Sir, the defendant cannot be here."

Prissy was clearly surprised and said indignantly:

"Well and just why not?" (Mistake, mistake, mistake.)

Mr. Warrington replied:

"Well, if you must know, Mr. Priscott, because poor young Jim is at death's door in the intensive care unit of Beebe Hospital with massive bleeding in his lower intestine. Lydia Mae was crying her heart out when she telephoned me to say the doctor's prognosis is guarded on several counts and that Jim could not possibly come to trial. I'll be glad to get an affidavit from Lydia Mae, or the attending physician, if you like. I'd also try to get Lydia Mae to come up from Felton, Delaware, if you want or need her, but she has no one to take care of her three youngsters" (one by Crazy Jim maybe and the other two by her former husband or a boyfriend, Mr. Warrington privately told me later).

Mr. Priscott replied somewhat dryly:

"No, no. That won't be at all necessary. We are all sorry to hear your client is indisposed, so to speak, Mr. Warrington. But what about the trucking company? Anyone here for them?"

Mr. Warrington replied, "Nope. The company went out of business long ago, sort of leaving my client, Jim, in the lurch, so to speak. Sorry, can't help you there, Mr. Priscott."

Mr. Warrington winked, but only to me, and said quietly to me as he sat back down, "Everything I said was true. Now, Prissy will have to use Crazy Jim's deposition. Jim testified on deposition that the Buick had stopped for no apparent reason quite suddenly when the yellow light came on. When our truck lightly tapped the rear bumper of the plaintiffs' Buick, the Buick lurched forward and then under its own power went all the way across through the intersection and ran into the fireplug. Jim also said that when the lady got out, she was cursing like a trooper at Mousey saying he had no business stopping at all and had not kept his foot on the brake. She told Jim the accident was all Mousey's fault. Jim also testified that she told him flat out that she wasn't hurt at all, just real mad at Mousey. I bet Prissy never mentions the trucking company again!"

Prissy then called the big lady plaintiff with the stiff white neck collar, as his first witness. Unfortunately for her (and for Prissy), she was obviously a nasty frump and came across just that way. Under Prissy's too prolonged questioning, she recounted in far too much fussy detail all about the drive down from their home near Bridgeport, Connecticut. She told us that she and "Mousey" were on their way to visit with her only niece who lived near Lynchburg, Virginia. Prissy got her to state in detail the intersection in Wilmington where this horrible accident had happened to her. She went on the describe in rehearsed detail how the defendant had slammed right into the back of their nice new Buick car, which was fully stopped in obedience to a yellow traffic light. She said that the Buick has been propelled by the truck all the way across the intersection and into a fireplug. She twisted her hankie and said that it was a mercy that she and "Mousey" had not suffered any broken bones or been cut or bruised. However, she more than made up for the lack of visible injuries by stating in reply to Prissy's detailed questions that she had suffered a whiplash injury for which she was forced to wear the big white neck collar she was so prominently displaying. She whined that her most serious injury, however, was "traumatic neurosis." She said that she could scarcely ever abide to ride in a car. Rolling her eyes piously toward heaven, she said she got the "willies," riding in a car even just to the Methodist Church which was only four and a half blocks from her house. Simply thinking about the intersection and the accident often made her weep. She proved her point by sniveling in her moist handkerchief right then and there. There had to be a recess so that she could regain her composure. On her return to the witness stand she said that, of course, she was still under her doctor's care. She was still taking medication and had to have weekly visits to the doctor for traumatic neurosis. She again dabbed her eyes with her handkerchief as she modestly admitted in some nice detail, in response to Prissy's delicate questioning, just why she was no longer able to perform her marital obligations for her husband as she had heretofore done with regularity and to their great pleasure and satisfaction. Her husband, Mr. Mousey, looked uncomfortable. The jury knew by common sense and experience that this tale of interrupted mid-life romance was exaggerated, if not downright litigation fantasy. Indeed, a couple of older country women on the jury looked outrightly skeptical at these alleged bedroom heroics.

However, all in all, this was pretty devastating stuff. I looked covertly over at the jury: some members at least were clearly sympathizing with the plaintiff.

Mr. Priscott then turned to Mr. Warrington and said with elaborate courtesy and a little bow, "Your witness, Mr. Warrington."

Mr. Warrington got somewhat heavily to his feet, with the help of his gold headed cane. He walked slowly over to the lectern. He paused, then turned and then said with gravity and courtesy to the frump on the stand.

"Madam, I doubt that you are very comfortable on the witness stand, particularly with that huge white neck collar that keeps your head and neck in place, right? Let me try to be very brief, unlike your able counsel, Mr. Priscott. I have only three questions to put to you. If you will be good enough to pay strict attention and answer my three questions truthfully, you will be off the witness stand very shortly. Okay? Are you ready? Let's begin.

"My first question in simple: Did you drive down yesterday with your husband from Connecticut for this trial?"

The lady's eyes rolled wildly around. Then she blurted out:

"No...Yes...But there was no train at the right time. Besides..."

Mr. Warrington let her flounder for a while. He then cut in firmly:

"No. Madam, please just answer my question. Did you drive here from Connecticut in a car driven by your husband? Please answer that question 'yes or no'. Then you can explain to the jury the reason you came by car in spite of your traumatic neurosis was because the trains of the Pennsylvania Railroad were not convenient to your schedule."

The plaintiff said in a low voice with downcast eyes: "Yes, we did drive down in our car."

Prissy whispered something feverishly to Ned. Ned nodded but made a little motion with his head indicating Prissy should be quiet.

Mr. Warrington savored that last answer for an additional moment to let it sink in. He then said, "Good. Now, let's turn to question No. 2. Ready?"

"In getting to the Hotel DuPont where you and your husband are staying, did you drive through the very intersection where the accident happened?"

Again, the lady looked up at the ceiling, than at the far wall of the Courtroom. She looked at Mr. Priscott for help: he was looking at the floor. Finally she said, "But there was no other way to get to the Hotel DuPont..."

Mr. Warrington looked pained and said:

"Ah, I see. But, Madam, you are unnecessarily prolonging my examination of you. I told you that I would ask only three questions. But, if I am to keep my end of the bargain and confine myself to three questions, you must help me and the jury by answering those questions and answering them directly and truthfully. Is that clear? Good. Let's try my second question again: It is a fact, is it not, that in driving down here and getting to the Hotel DuPont, you came right through the very intersection that you have told us in such exquisite detail is a source of your 'traumatic neurosis', vivid dreams, weeping, and all that stuff? Please answer that 'yes or no'. Then perhaps you can inform the jury as to why you think that there is only one street in Wilmington that leads to the Hotel DuPont."

After a long pause, the lady said in a subdued voice, "Yes sir. We did come through that intersection."

Ned frowned imperceptibly. Prissy got halfway to his feet but Ned tapped his arm and he sat back down.

Mr. Warrington let the jury think about that answer for a little while. Then Mr. Warrington said:

"How about that! Well, then, now let's get to my third and last question. My final question to you is simple: tell all of us exactly what traumatic neurosis is."

The lady looked perplexed and thought for quite a while. She then said cautiously, "Well, I am not real sure I can tell you exactly what it is but my Hartford doctor tells me it's what I've got as a result of this terrible accident."

Mr. Warrington looked pained and said, "Madam, I, the Court, and the members of this jury all know that you claim that you have traumatic neurosis. But what I want to know is, *what is it?* Just tell us plainly in your own words so we can all understand just what traumatic neurosis is."

There was a long silence and then the lady said:

"I don't know really what traumatic neurosis is. All I know is that I am told that I have it and that I have it as a result of the accident."

Then she added in a snipy and belligerent tone, "So, there. That's my answer for you, Mr. Warrington." (Mistake, mistake, msitake!) Ned winced. I glanced at Mousey: I got the distinct impression that along with everyone else Mousey was secretly enjoying seeing his overbearing wife's discomfiture.

Mr. Warrington said, "Why, thank you, madam, you have been quite informative in your own way in helping me and the jury in getting to the bottom of your claim of traumatic neurosis. Your Honor, I have no further questions for the plaintiff." He sat down. Ned looked grave. Prissy looked perplexed.

There was a recess. I asked Mr. Warrington how he had known that the plaintiff and her husband had driven down and how she had come through the intersection. Mr. Warrington offered me a Lucky Strike, which I of course accepted. He lit our cigarettes with a blue kitchen match which he struck on the seat of his pants. He replied:

"Sonny, when I got to the Hotel DuPont, I saw a little Buick sitting there with Connecticut plates. It had a little dent in its rear bumper. I put two and two together. I took a chance on the second question. I bet that the husband would have come through the same intersection since it in fact is the best street to get to the Hotel DuPont."

I then asked, "Well, how did you know to ask her what traumatic neurosis is?" Mr. Warrington replied, "Well, Sonny Boy, I don't know what traumatic neurosis is. I don't suppose that even a smart young fellow like you right out of Harvard Law School or anybody on that jury has ever heard of it before. So, I thought that I just might ask her. It turns out that she, like the rest of us, doesn't know. But, you can be right sure Ned and Prissy know. They will undoubtedly tell us with the help of their famous Hartford psychiatrist. But, that is not the same as if the plaintiff knew and told the jury, now is it, Sonny Boy?"

Well the trial went on. Ned's fastidious colleague, Prissy, insisted on calling not one but both Wilmington policemen. They testified after consulting their laboriously handwritten notes and the official traffic report that the defendant's truck had in fact come up to the traffic light, did not stop, and then and there did rear end the car of party Number 2 from Connecticut and pushed the said car 17 feet, 6 inches, in a northeasterly direction across the intersection where it ended up 3.19 inches, from the curb, and against an (innocent) fireplug that just happened to be there, etc. etc. Mr. Warrington asked me to cross-examine the two policemen, saying each time as he clapped me on the back, "Go get 'em Tiger." I did cross-examine at great length and with great enthusiasm but with absolutely no effect whatsoever except to bore the hell out of the jury by too precise establishment of all these irrelevant petty details. The jury's annoyance was compounded when Prissy insisted on calling two eyewitnesses who also testified ad nauseam under Prissy's detailed questions (and my interminable cross) about the incontrovertible fact that the big bad chicken truck had indeed struck the plaintiff's car from behind, and that it had gone across the intersection and into the innocent fireplug, etc. We rehashed these now stale and uncontested facts and measurements with all the intensity, sarcasm, posturing, and incredulity that two lawyers from Harvard Law School can muster, seeking to impress the jury. Mr. Warrington himself nodded in his seat. At least two of the jurors snored audibly during all of this useless infighting.

During the afternoon recess, I asked Mr. Warrington why he did not just admit liability and be done with it. It was perfectly clear in spite of my valiant efforts on cross-examination of the police, Mousey, and the eyewitnesses and Crazy Jim's deposition that our driver had come up to the light, had not stopped, and had hit the plaintiff's car in the rear. Mr. Warrington said, "Sonny Boy, I thought some about admitting liability but then I thought, maybe, just maybe, Prissy might just bore the almighty hell out of this long-suffering jury by proving over and over what the jury understood from the opening." Mr. Warrington went on to remark that juror Number 2 had had a nice nap all afternoon long and that Numbers 3 and 7 seemed irritated. Mr. Warrington concluded with a sly smile, "Could be things are looking somewhat up. Sonny Boy, your father once told me that he never wins cases: other people just lose them. Well, Prissy may be in a fair way of doing just that. We'll just have to hope Ned does not get a chance to correct the damage Prissy has already managed to do to his nice little plaintiff's case."

Prissy had said in his opening that this case was really about damages and the extent of the plaintiff's grievous injuries. Prissy then called a nurse from the emergency ward of what was then the old Delaware Hospital. This crusty old Emergency Ward nurse made it quite clear that she was highly exasperated at having to come to Court to testify in this partcular case. She testified that the plaintiff had been brought in after the accident on a stretcher, had been examined, x-rayed and released. Mr. Warrington elected to handle this cross-examination himself. He established again in three questions that, after an examination and a couple of x-rays the plaintiff had been released, that she had walked out of the Emergency Room on her own two feet and in fact had walked all the way over to the Hotel DuPont and that she had never come back for the scheduled follow-up examination and medicine the next day. Her total medical expenses (other than for weekly visits to her psychiatrist) came to only $131.00. (I noted that Mousey half smiled.)

At the end of the first day, Mr. Warrington lit up a Lucky Strike, gave me one, and allowed that he felt sort of tired. I asked whether I could take any portion of his file, so that I could review it that night (and put it in some sort of order). Mr. Warrington replied, "You can have the whole damn file: I certainly don't need any of those papers tonight. Please give back my Thucydides. But, what I do really need is a drink of rye whiskey. Would you care to join me?" Indeed, I did. We walked over to the Hotel DuPont bar and had a drink together. I left Mr. Warrington there, ordering yet another Maryland Rye Whisky on the rocks and chain-smoking Lucky Strike cigarettes. I went dutifully back to the office. I asked my father just who Thucydides was and what the Peloponnesian Wars were.

"Good God," my father exclaimed in real surprise. "I have paid literally a small-size fortune for your four years at Princeton, and you have never even heard of the world's greatest historian. What did you learn there besides how to drink beer? I guess you think that some familiarity with the filthy books of that Irish expatriate, James Joyce, makes you an educated person, right?"

I replied smugly, "Well, I guess I am better educated than Mr. Warrington who, I believe, went to a little unknown law school that I at least have never heard of, called, I believe, St. James."

My father roared with laughter. "My dear boy, St. James is one of the oldest colleges at Oxford University. Mr. Warrington was an early Rhodes Scholar from Delaware. He was at Oxford before I was and graduated in law in 1911. So, there, Mister Smarty Pants: put that in your pipe and smoke it. Incidentally, you just might some time read Thucydides—not in Greek, it goes without saying. You just might find it interesting and instructive."

Considerably humbled and now in real awe of Mr. Warrington, I spent until midnight reviewing and organizing the file for whatever good that might do. Clearly, on the following day, the preliminaries being over, we were going to have to face the traumatic music, so to speak. Ned and Prissy had scheduled their fancy Hartford psychiatrist to come all the way down to Wilmington and testify as to the plaintiff's traumatic neurosis. We had a report from this distinguished Connecticut doctor flatly stating that the plaintiff's traumatic neurosis was the result of the accident. The doctor concluded that she unfortunately would never for the rest of her natural life be the same gentle, pleasant, loving wife and homemaker she had been before the accident. I trembled as I read this most damaging report: it certainly looked like there was going to be a verdict of tidal proportions against us.

The next day, I joined Mr. Warrington at 10:00 A.M. He was seated at the defense table with his cane between his knees. His eyes were closed. He was either in deep thought or fast asleep. Two crushed Lucky Strike butts lay at his feet. The trial got underway. With great formality, Prissy called the Hartford psychiatrist: the doctor was bald headed, had a neatly trimmed reddish Van Dyke beard, and little beady eyes behind steel rim glasses. He was very intense and serious. He spoke with just a touch of Germanic accent but without the faintest glimmer of humor. His six-page, single-spaced resume or curriculum vitae was made a trial exhibit. Mr. Warrington looked at our copy of this impressive document very briefly and then openly turned it over on the table in front of him, making certain that the jury saw him do it. At this point, I was afraid Mr. Warrington would again turn to me for the cross-examination of this distinguished and assured witness. I therefore covertly examined the vita carefully. I saw nothing at all on which I could attack the doctor. Prissy's examination started with a review of the great man's career. The doctor had attended prominent medical schools in Germany and Austria. The recitation of his list of medical societies and committees, the books and papers he had written, the grants that he had received and the honors heaped on his bald head took half an hour in itself. Mr. Warrington appeared to be napping while Prissy went over the doctor's resume. Then the doctor was examined in great detail on traumatic neurosis generally: we all knew then that at least Prissy knew exactly what traumatic neurosis was: he suavely testified about traumatic neurosis long and lovingly. (Of course, it was his "bread and butter".) I wondered how Mr. Warrington was going to deal with this distinguished expert who had testified so knowledgeably and so convincingly. I shuddered at the thought that Mr. Warrington, whose attention clearly seemed to be elsewhere, would turn and ask me to take the doctor on in cross-examination.

Eventually, Prissy finished and said, again with a little bow and great politeness, "Your witness, Mr. Warrington." His tone clearly implied that Mr. Warrington would not be able to do anything with such a great medical authority. Mr. Warrington stood up (thank God) and, while walking over to the podium, said "By the way, Professor, you a real doctor?" The witness bristled visibly at this insult and retorted fiercely, his Germanic accent becoming more pronounced, "Ja or rather yes, of course I am: we have just been over my credentials." Mr. Warrington replied evenly: "Hold on, don't get yourself in an uproar. Everybody heard all your lengthy credentials. But I was not quite sure that you are still a real medical doctor or whether you had become just a professor of some sort at this point." Prissy at this point objected and was sustained.

Mr. Warrington said: "I see, Doctor, you are something of an expert on rats."

The doctor again visibly bristled: "No, not on der rats. I am a psychiatrist and treat humans, not rats." His Germanic accent became more pronounced.

Mr. Warrington, "Why, Doctor, your vita says right here that you got a three-year grant to do a study for the U.S. Department of Health entitled 'Empiric Studies on the Emotional and Sexual Behavior of Male Rats in Three-Rat Combinations'."

The doctor nodded, "Ja, so?"

Mr. Warrington said, "Doctor, just how much money did you get over the three years from the United States Treasury for your studies of the romantic doings of male rats?"

The jury was convulsed. (Even Mousey smirked.)

Prissy jumped to his feet in spite of Ned's attempt to restrain him, "We object, Your Honor. These questions are not relevant and are highly improper!"

Mr. Warrington responded gently, "But, Your Honor, Mr. Priscott himself has just put the good doctor's vita in evidence. Surely, I am entitled to a few ratty questions, so to speak."

The Court, attempting itself to cover its own amusement, ruled: "Objection overruled. You may proceed briefly, Mr. Warrington." The Court could not resist a "funny" of its own: "But, let's all remember this is not a trial about the emotional and sexual behavior of rats a number of years ago."

Mr. Warrington said, "Very well, Your Honor. Now, how much did you get to study and report on rat sex, doctor?"

The doctor was plainly a trifle rattled (so to speak) and finally said, "Maybe $15-20,000."

Mr. Warrington, "Per year, Doctor?"

Doctor, "Of course."

Mr. Warrington, "Well, Doctor, you certainly are a worthy successor of that former German rat doctor, the great Pied Piper of Hamlin."

But the Court plainly had had enough of Mr. Warrington's playing cat and mouse with the doctor and said, "Mr. Warrington, enough of this. Do you have any serious questions to put to this witness?"

Mr. Warrington continued, "Ah, yes, indeed I do, Your Honor. Doctor, bear with me. I know from your charges how valuable your time is. I am just a country lawyer from lower Delaware trying to do my job for my client, Jim, who really is sick and may be dying at this very moment. Okay? I can only afford about three minutes of your precious time. Thus, I will ask you only three questions. Please pay strict attention and answer my three questions truthfully." (The jury clearly knew what was coming: they became instantly attentive and sat forward on the edges of their seats.) The doctor looked puzzled: he instinctively smelled a rat but he did not know what was coming. Mr. Warrington paused for a moment and said, "Well now, Doctor, tell us all when it was that you last treated someone with a broken bone or you last stitched a kid up who had cut his leg, or treated a housewife who burned herself while cooking."

The doctor said, slightly uncomfortably: "Vell, now, let's see. That would have been way back ven I was in medical school back in Vienna in the 1920s, or perhaps ven I was a young intern in Bremen. But, I haven't done any of that ordinary sort of medicine in the last thirty years or so." Mr. Warrington said, "I see."

The doctor then turned directly to the Judge and said somewhat fiercely: "Your Honor, what's all this got to do with this case? Your Honor, I came all der way here to Wilmington to testify on traumatic neurosis, not common everyday household injuries or rats." Mistake, mistake, mistake! The jury was not impressed. The Court said impassively, "Doctor, please answer Mr. Warrington's questions."

Mr. Warrington said reflectively, "Oh, I see. You haven't treated visible injuries for some thirty years. You treat the invisible injuries?"

Prissy objected again to Ned's disguised dismay. The Court overruled him. "This is cross-examination, Mr. Priscott."

Mr. Warrington: "Second question. Now, tell us, Doctor, has this lady improved at all in the year and a half she has been coming to you for treatment every single week for a half-hour visit?"

The doctor paused nervously, obviously undecided which way to jump. He took off his glasses and polished them with his white handkerchief. Finally, he said with fine German deliberation, "No, as a matter of fact, she has not improved at all. She has der permanent condition. She will need my help, guidance, and support for a very long time."

Mr. Warrington: "Third and final question, Doctor, what do you charge this unfortunate patient of yours for a half-hour visit?"

The doctor said uncomfortably, "Well, my normal charge should be $200.00 per visit, but I am only charging her $180.00 per visit." Some of the jury looked shocked, incredulous, or disturbed.

Mr. Warrington said, "Well, Doctor, it would be a pity for you, I guess, if she ever got better, right?" Before the doctor could answer or Prissy sputter another objection, Mr. Warrington said, "Your Honor, that last question is withdrawn. No further questions, Herr Doctor, thank you."

In spite of Mr. Warrington's devastating "three questions," I worried about what effect this distinguished doctor would have on our Delaware jury. This Germanic psychiatrist had been pretty impressive. But Mr. Warrington had a medical ace up his sleeve: an elderly doctor of his own. It turned out that our doctor was a plain old fashioned American doctor who had grown up in Felton, Delaware. He had worked at the Delaware State Mental Hospital for some thirty-three years. I am sure some of the jury had had family members who had been treated and helped by our medical witness. Our doctor was of the conservative school: he didn't believe one damn bit in traumatic neurosis and said so. (I noticed that he also wore black boots that laced up to his ankles.) He testified under Mr. Warrington's questioning that traumatic neurosis was either self-induced or could be induced and indeed prolonged by doctors who claimed that an indefinite program of expensive weekly visits was necessary. He concluded by saying in his opinion the lady would be quite her old self again once this case was over, no matter what the outcome.

The testimony was all in by the end of the second day. We then had a prayer conference. Ned and Prissy handed the Court the original and two copies of carefully prepared prayers (or Requests to Charge) with citations to all the cases and authorities. Mr. Warrington told the Judge that the defendant would be quite content with the Court's usual charge on negligence, burden of proof, damages, consortium, credibility, etc. Thus, Ned and Prissy virtually wrote the Judge's charge. I told Mr. Warrington that the plaintiffs had had the better of us on what was going to go into the Judge's charge to the jury. Mr. Warrington replied evenly, "Sonny Boy, maybe in the Harvard Law School classrooms the charge is important. But, I have found that a Delaware jury can't be expected to hear and understand the niceties of the law when it is read to them by the Judge, especially after lunch. Besides, most juries have too much common sense to decide a case based on what the Judge and the lawyers say the law is. The system works as well as it does for that very reason: the jury brings its collective sense of reality to bear on the case and decides that way, no matter what the Court says in its so-called charge. Thus, the jury comes out right in most cases. That is the real reason why we still need juries. Prayers and the charge are the legal folderol of lawyers and judges. The charge is the basis of 90% of the appeals. But, you and I, Sonny Boy, if we win this case in this connection, have got to make damn sure Ned and Prissy have no basis for an appeal, right?" I replied "Right," quite firmly. Privately, I thought Mr. Warrington had gone bonkers if he thought he was going to win this particular case.

Again, Mr. Warrington invited me up to the Brandywine Room for a little snort at the end of the day. As he sat down and lit up a Lucky with a kitchen match which he struck with his thumbnail, I asked Mr. Warrington how he thought the case was going. He replied noncommittally: "Okay, I guess." Actually, though Mr. Warrington had scored some counterpunches, the plaintiff's case had gone in like clockwork. Prissy had gone from one of Ned's big black notebooks to another, ticking off all the points. When asked, I told Mr. Warrington frankly that I thought we were going to get a good shellacking. I asked Mr.

Warrington if he had recommended any settlement to the insurance company. Mr. Warrington replied: "No, Sonny Boy, of course, I did not. I am paid to defend cases. Any nincompoop can give the insurance company's money away in cases like this one. That just makes everybody's auto insurance premiums go up for no good reason at all. This lady doesn't have one goddamn thing wrong with her really. Of course, she probably imagines she does. She is encouraged in this fantasy by the whole litigation process and by that bearded disciple of Dr. Freud from Hartford."

He then went on: "Now, Billy Boy, you've been a real help to me in this case. But, I'm getting too old to do this sort of thing. It sort of wears me down. Could you prepare and give the closing argument to the jury? I may read a few pages of Thucydides this evening." I set my glass down. I thanked Mr. Warrington for the drink and for the honor he had done me in giving me the responsibility of the closing. I hurried back to the office. I wrote out the closing as carefully as I could. I memorized it. I then rehearsed it before my mirror. Indeed, I rehearsed it again the following morning before my father. My father was most doubtful that we had any chance at all. He gruffly allowed that my closing was reasonably adequate considering the poverty of what we had to go on both as to liability and damages. He said gloomily as I left, "Well, good luck, my boy."

I got to Court. It looked like Mr. Warrington had had a bad evening. He looked very old and tired. Ned bounced into Court, full of energy. Prissy minced in. His plaintiff lady looked like it was Christmas morning and she was going to go down to open her presents under the tree. (Even Mr. Mousey looked quite perky: new Buick?) Mousey said good morning to me in a friendly sort of manner.

In due course, the Judge came on the Bench. He asked if we were ready to give our closings. We were. The jury was ushered in and seated. Prissy got up and nervously gave a closing in his high pitched voice from typed notes covering all the points in precise detail, making it exquisitely clear once again that there simply could be no doubt about liability. Of course, Prissy spent the bulk of his time pointing out the plaintiff's injuries and damages, including, of course, traumatic neurosis. He even mentioned Mr. Mousey's loss of consortium and the $179.50 for repairs to the Buick. He sat down. I then got up. I recited in a half-apologetic manner my little closing. I skipped over liability, not even mentioning the damning admissions that Mousey had made as to both liability and damages in his deposition, which Prissy had himself introduced. I then talked a little bit about the lady's injuries and the damages, trying as best I could to minimize them. Then, I sat down.

Prissy then had the right to make a reply to my closing, though nothing that I had been able to say merited much by way of reply, but just as Prissy got to his feet, Mr. Warrington hoisted himself to his feet with the aid of his cane. He said to the Court, "Your Honor, my young friend here from Harvard Law School has done right well in closing to the jury, especially as this is his very first jury trial. I am proud to have been associated with him in this trial. However, it seems to me as an old attorney that he may have overlooked or not touched on a few things. I wonder if the Court and plaintiffs' counsel would do me the courtesy of permitting me to say just a few words at this point to the jury." The Court looked over at Mr. Carpenter and Mr. Priscott and said doubtfully, "Well, it's a little bit irregular to have two attorneys for the defendant participate in a closing, but if Mr. Carpenter and Mr. Priscott have no objection, then I don't see any reason why not." After conferring a moment with Mr. Priscott (who clearly was vehemently opposed), Mr. Carpenter stood up and said (gracious to a fault), "Why, of course, Your Honor, the plaintiffs have no objection, Your Honor." (Mistake, mistake, mistake!)

Mr. Warrington then walked slowly over in front of the jury, leaning on his gold headed cane. He began speaking in his great rasping, booming voice. He reviewed the whole damn case right from start to finish. He emphasized the fact that Crazy Jim's deposition testimony showed that the accident had happened according to the plaintiff herself, because Mousey had stopped suddenly for a yellow light and had let his foot slip off the brake when the Buick was rear ended. Mr. Warrington also drove home the point that the plaintiff herself had said she was not hurt at the scene and had walked out of the Emergency Room on her own two feet and had never come back. The jury and indeed everyone in the courtroom listened to him with rapt attention, mesmerized like mice before a swaying cobra. Mr. Warrington's gestures, his every inflection fascinated each and every person in that courtroom, including the Judge himself. About half an hour later, Mr. Warrington concluded in a swelling climax: "Members of the jury, like some of you, I am a plain sort of fellow. I was raised down in Sussex County where my dear old father, may he rest in peace, worked as a poor farmer. We were also the part owners of a little country general store near Hollyville. One summer day, when I was about nine years, my old pa told me that when I was tending our general store not just to take a quarter that a customer offered without carefully examining it to see if it was genuine. My father said, 'Son, flip the quarter in the air. Listen to its ring, then, slap it down on the counter. If the quarter sings in the air and slaps down true, then put it in the register. However, if it has a phony lead sound and does not ring true when it hits the counter, why, then shove that counterfeit quarter right back to the customer.'

Well, members of the jury, in this traumatic neurosis case Billy Boy and I have sort of tried to flip this case in the air for you." He took his thumb and flipped an imaginary quarter high in the air. The jury's eyes watched the invisible coin spiral upward. They watched as Mr. Warrington slapped the invisible coin down on the counsel table, then hit the counsel table smartly with his cane. His red face was flushed with anger as he thundered like an Old Testament prophet, "Members of the jury, we've all had to sit there and listen to this traumatic neurosis clap-trap for three whole days. Like that slug that was offered to me so many years ago when I was a kid down in Sussex County, this case does not ring true. Now that you have heard the case, does traumatic neurosis ring true to you? No, of course it certainly does not. Since it does not ring true, send it back to the lady plaintiff and her phony German doctor." Then, pausing and changing and softening his tone and manner. Mr. Warrington continued. "But, members of the jury, don't be harsh; don't be mean: be sympathetic and kindly. In spite of everything, perhaps you should allow the $100 for the shaking up she got in the accident. Also, you just might give her $131.00 for the out-of-pocket expenses for the medical expenses she really did pay. Throw in $179.00 for the Buick's dented bumper. But, don't, don't for pity sake encourage this sort of snake oil medicine by paying her and the Pied Piper from Hartford for the so-called traumatic neurosis or loss of consortium. Thank you." Ned smiled wanly during these last remarks. There was silence: you could have heard the proverbial pin drop. Then the jury (and indeed the bailiffs) sort of half broke into applause. Mr. Warrington walked slowly back to his seat and sat down, breathing heavily. The Judge tapped his gavel but not forcefully—he too was still under the spell of Mr. Warrington's oratory. Mr. Warrington mopped the perspiration from his red face with a soiled blue bandanna which he pulled from his back pocket. He said in an aside to me, "Now, that's what I get paid for." But, I was taken aback: why didn't Mr. Warrington go for broke and demand a defendants' verdict. (I certainly would have.)

Prissy had the right to reply and did so, but, after Mr. Warrington, it was difficult for Prissy to say anything at all, much less anything that would overcome Mr. Warrington's awesome performance.

The Court then gave its charge to the jury. As Mr. Warrington predicted, the jurymen dozed or looked glass-eyed. Prissy scribbled notes furiously. Mr. Warrington surreptitiously brought out a big black jackknife and pared his nail underneath the counsel table. I tried to pay attenton as the Court droned on. Eventually, the jury filed out.

But, the jury was back in less than half an hour. They gave the lady $100.00 general damages plus $131.00, her medical expenses other than for the bills for the traumatic neurosis treatment. The jury did not give one red cent for pain and suffering, nor a penny for traumatic neurosis and for her traumatic neurosis doctor bills, just as Mr. Warrington suggested. They gave Mr. Mousey $171 for his dented bumper, but not a cent for consortium he had never lost. The Court smiled benignly, thanking the jury for its service. (The Court knew that the ends of justice had been served that day at least.)

When the jury had retired, Ned came right over and courteously congratulated Mr. Warrington (and me) on the trial and the result. Mr. Warrington replied to Ned's congratulations, "Fleet and Army perished from the face of the earth: nothing was saved, and of many who set out, few returned home. These were the events in Sicily." Ned replied somewhat ruefully, "The end of the Athenian expedition to Syracuse: Thucydides really knew how to describe a defeat." The lady plaintiff spat out, "Goddamn you, Mr. Warrington, you can go right straight to hell for all I care." Mr. Mousey suppressed another little smile behind his wife's big back. Prissy said nothing but scowled as he packed up the briefcases.

Mr. Warrington and I puffed on Lucky Strikes. Mr. Warrington lit our cigarettes with a blue kitchen match which he struck on the counsel table. When the "Athenians" left, he clapped me on the back and said, "Well, thanks, Sonny Boy, for all your assistance. You were a real help. Guess we showed them, right? Wish we had time for a victory drink or two." I asked him, "Mr. Warrington, why didn't you ask the jury for a defendant's verdict?" Mr. Warrington winked and said, "No time to explain now, Sonny Boy. Ask your father—he'll know. Mr. Carpenter also knows, but, poor old Prissy is too damn dumb to figure that one out" (as indeed I was as well).

Mr. Warrington then left right away saying that he had a manslaughter case starting the next morning in Sussex County and that he had to prepare that case.

I heard later that Prissy became a law professor—"Those who can do, those who can't teach." Two or three years after the trial, Mousey wrote me a nice note from Florida right out of the blue. His wife had indeed discarded her neck collar on the drive back to Hartford and had never gone back to the doctor. Mercifully for Mousey, she had died of a stroke about a year later. Mousey had since married a nice hairdresser and moved to Rondo Bay, Florida, where he was doing well, thank you.

Ned had uncharacteristically left his spiral notebook behind him on the counsel table. His last note said, "'Sonny Boy' never will be a threat, not a chip off the old block—a pebble maybe? But, never, never again agree to letting two lawyers participate in a closing, especially when one is Everett Warrington." Right, right, right!

I hurried back to our office, triumphant and wreathed in smiles, though I had precious little to do with this incredible result. To my father's profound irritation, I lit up a Lucky Strike. (I burned my thumb as I have many times since then trying to light a blue match with my thumbnail.) My father listened and somewhat grudgingly felicitated me for having participated in a trial with such a wonderful outcome. He warned me about hubris. Then I asked with real puzzlement why Mr. Warrington had not asked the jury for a defendant's verdict. My father replied, "What a goose you are! The reason is obvious. Since the jury has brought in a verdict for the plaintiffs, there is no way that Ned and Mr. Priscott can appeal, can they?" Of course: that explained Ned's wan smile.

Then my father said, "Well, and what did you really learn?" I recounted my glowing admiration for Mr. Warrington's tour de force: he had asked only nine questions in cross-examination and won the case by a rousing closing. My father smiled: "I do not wonder that you are impressed with Everett's virtuoso style. As I told you, there is no one at the Delaware Bar who is better with a jury, as you yourself have just seen. You have, however, failed to understand Everett's crafty strategy. Prissy, as Everett called Mr. Priscott, himself ruined the case for the plaintiffs. Also, Everett got you to scrap endlessly with Mr. Priscott over the details. Ned never had a chance to control the case. I assure you Ned would never have handled the case ineptly if he had not had to defer to his out-of-town counsel whose case it was. But, young man, nine times out of ten, and particularly in substantial litigation, Ned's careful preparation on the law and the facts will pay off. Ned's six black notebooks with the tabs that you now deride because you were present when Ned's colleague managed to lose a small inconsequential personal injury case evidences an orderly approach and system that will succeed in substantial litigation in the years to come. Before you go and try to win a jury trial by asking only nine questions or banging on counsel tables with a ruler during closing, think carefully about the contrasting styles you have just seen. Mark my words: Ned will surely become one of Delaware's ablest trial lawyers. Everett Warrington is certainly a colorful trial lawyer from Sussex County. But, unfortunately, Everett Warrington has wasted his gifts and his life: he will leave no lasting mark in Delaware legal history. He tries cases like this one mostly for his own fun and to pass the time away. No, indeed, you would do far better to model yourself on Ned than to try to ape Everett's firehouse style. Also, you would do well to read Thucydides so that you know what the reference to 'an expedition to Syracuse' means the next time it comes up."

As always, my father was right. (In those days, we did as we were told.) I have tried ineffectually to follow in Ned's footsteps. Thus, I have indeed read Thucydides with pleasure and edification. But out of affectionate respect and remembrance for Everett F. Warrington, Esquire, I sometimes wear red suspenders on Tuesdays.

"*If we shadows have offended,*
*Think but this, and all is mended—*
*That you have but slumb'red here*
*While these visions did appear.*
*And this weak and idle theme,*
*No more yielding but a dream,*
*Gentles, do not reprehend.*
*If you pardon, we will mend.*
*And, as I am an honest Puck,*
*If we have unearned luck*
*Now to scape the serpent's tongue,*
*We will make amends ere long;*
*Else a Puck a liar call.*
*So, good night unto you all.*
*Give me your hands, if we be friends,*
*And Robin shall restore amends.*"

*A Midsummer Night's Dream*
Act V
Scene 1

# Colophon

This book was composed in 9 point Century Schoolbook, two point leaded. It was printed by the Cedar Tree Press on special-made 100# acid-free Curtis Tweedweave Text manufactured by the Curtis Paper Company in its Newark, Delaware mill. It was bound by Advantage Bookbinding of Baltimore, Maryland, in full cloth, with Curtis Tweedweave endleaves.